FENG SHUI
For Hawai'i

FENG SHUI
For Hawai'i

CLEAR ENGLEBERT

WATERMARK
PUBLISHING

ISBN 978-0-9796769-9-4

Library of Congress Control Number: 2008934936

Design
Gonzalez Design Co.

Production
Marisa Oshiro

Watermark Publishing
1088 Bishop St., Suite 310
Honolulu, Hawaii 96813
Telephone 1-808-587-7766
Toll-free 1-866-900-BOOK
sales@bookshawaii.net
www.bookshawaii.net

Printed in China

Contents

Introduction

This book concerns the most common feng shui problems in and around Hawai'i homes. It is about the flow of energy, called *chi* (or *qi*) in China and *ki* in Japan. Energy flow is the basis of the oldest kind of feng shui, known as Form School or Landform Feng Shui. It is concerned with the form of things: the form of the furniture and its arrangement, the actual form of the house and the form of the land around the house. In Hawai'i the land around the house is sometimes quite dramatic—the *pali* on one side and the Pacific Ocean on the other. Both can offer feng shui challenges depending on their proximity. Even a less-spectacular location can have an unbalanced feel based on the home's *mauka* and *makai* situation.

Homes in Hawai'i are often set up to maximize a nice view and to take advantage of cooling breezes. That degree of openness (so many big holes in the walls) can offer opportunities for *chi* to leave too quickly. In some instances, the home scarcely holds energy at all—it's all about the view. *Chi* flow in feng shui can be understood in three ways: the actual flow of air and sunlight into the home, the flow of where we can easily go between and within rooms (designers call this the traffic flow within the home) and the direction our eyes and attention move to—what we notice—along the way. People have *chi* energy. The things we notice affect us, often subtly, even subconsciously. Feng shui maintains that our "attentive energy" (what we are paying attention to) is shaping our lives.

Even when we're not looking out a window, here in Hawai'i the decorative objects and furniture we choose often say "tropics." Deciding which things to live with and have near to us is a major point in feng shui. Often I see pictures of a single *hula* dancer in the home of a single person, and

The word for wind is *feng*, and pronounced "fung." The moving wind is a form of energy, or *chi*.

I'll suggest instead a picture of the *hālau* (dance troupe) to symbolize togetherness and doing something *with* other people. On the other hand, too many *objects* can create clutter, a problematic situation in feng shui. Clutter's big in Hawai'i, but this book doesn't dwell on it because, if it did, you would probably put it right back down. Instead, it is covered under Gifts (guess why?), and the section is short, sweet and to the point. Some "tropical look" furniture has curved edges of bamboo or rattan palm and is considered to be a friendly choice for the flow of *chi* energy. However, some furniture (especially some glass tabletops) has what's called cutting energy (*shar chi*). Open beams often have cutting energy, and so do most ceiling fans.

A picture of several dancers, rather than just one, creates a feeling of togetherness, not loneliness.

SOLUTIONS

When you notice a feng shui problem, then the challenge is to come up with workable solutions. There are two kinds of solutions: real ones and symbolic ones. Real solutions fix the problem and change the situation. The degree of change necessary is often not feasible, so there are symbolic solutions, ones that simply symbolize a change. You may try more than one solution if you desire, because different solutions often represent different approaches to the problem. I recommend saying out loud why you are engaging in the symbolic solution at the moment that you do so. The solution is thereby strengthened. I think of homes as physical prayers or requests that signal what kinds of things we'd like to have happen in our lives—such as harmonious relationships, good health and abundance.

Sometimes the object that represents the solution doesn't look good in the home—perhaps it clashes with the décor. In that case the solution can be hidden. You can hide mirrors behind pictures, or put crystals in baskets. As long as it's there, it's working for you.

Some feng shui solutions are the kind that you do once and that's it—you can forget about the problem and go on with your happy life. Other solutions involve changing a habit, such as not bringing more clutter into the house, or remembering to close the toilet lid.

No feng shui book is truly comprehensive, because there's always going to be some new situation that you never could have imagined. One of the things that make this book unique is that it offers multiple solutions. What good is it to know about a problem if the solution isn't feasible? If you've ever read a feng shui book, you know that most of them offer one solution per problem and move on to the next, giving you the impression that that's the only way to deal with the issue. There's almost always more than one way to solve an undesirable situation, depending on your style and circumstances, and this book gives you those options. To me, that's the art of feng shui.

That's how I think of feng shui: as an art, like decorating. The system of rules that comprises feng shui may not be classified as a science in the modern sense, but it teaches us to consciously notice where our attention is being drawn and what symbols are around us. This is a cross-cultural belief. Winston Churchill once said, "We shape our buildings; thereafter they shape us."

Feng shui looks at the shape of the land to determine the flow of energy. In feng shui terms, the prosperity of O'ahu is protected by a dragon, symbolized by the jagged spine of the Ko'olaus. The island is fortunate indeed to have such auspicious beauty.

This was also an important concept in old Hawai'i. The title of the person who was consulted before building a house or temple was *kuhikuhi pu'uone* ("the one who points out contours"). Likewise, one of the most important things a feng shui consultant does is to point out the contours around a home or potential building site, explaining their symbolism. I feng shui'd for a man in Ola'a, and partway through the consultation he said, "This reminds me of what my Hawaiian grandfather used to say, but I was just a kid and didn't pay attention." We both wished he could remember more. In ancient China, they wrote down their philosophy and methods, and then they printed their writings, so there has been ample opportunity to spread and adapt the art form.

I hope this book will inspire you to adapt feng shui to your own unique circumstances in the Islands. It begins with the outside, then moves inside the front door and takes a look at how the home is built. Finally there are chapters on furniture and decorative objects, the things that we've brought into our homes, and how they are affecting us. I believe that learning more about this ancient discipline can help us in our modern-day lives to achieve our goals. Though the situations may change, the principles of the art—and our own hopes and desires—remain the same. ✑

EXTERIOR

The official front door is of primary importance because it is the "mouth of chi." It represents the opportunity for good energy to enter your life. This is often where a feng shui consultation begins.

Mauka or *Makai* Front Door

The strongest buildings have their official front door on the *makai* (seaward) side. In feng shui, a *mauka* (towards the mountain) orientation symbolizes protection—if the mountain is behind your home. If it is in front, it symbolizes an obstacle: Life is an uphill battle. The ocean symbolizes abundance, and it should be in front of your house, as if you could harvest its bounty through the front door. If it is behind, the ocean symbolizes the abyss: The house has no backing and is slipping downhill. This situation is especially severe in homes that are right on the ocean or next to a steep gulch. The most preferable solution in this instance is to move, but that's certainly not feasible for most folks. Luckily, there are plenty of symbolic solutions for a front door on the *mauka* side of the building.

Left: The mountain is behind the house, symbolizing strength and protection. The front door is on the *makai* side.

Previous Spread: The front door is often one of the first places *chi* approaches your house—make it welcoming!

Opposite: A water feature can symbolically change the orientation of a building so that the abundance of *wai* enters the house.

SOLUTIONS

Outside the Front

The first three solutions are outside, visible in front of the home. First impressions are the most powerful. They create 90 percent of long-lasting impressions. Solutions noticed first thing are usually quite strong.

• Put a **weathervane** on top of the roof. It should be centered on the roof and be noticeable as you approach the home. The weathervane moves; movement attracts attention; attention is energy—so energy is pulled upward as one approaches the home. The image on the weathervane is also important. A flying bird such as a crane is perfect. It lifts the energy even more. An airplane is also fine. The image of a water creature such as a whale, dolphin or fish isn't recommended in this instance because they live below the water and don't have the same "lifting" symbolism as a bird. If a weathervane isn't feasible, you can approximate this solution by having anything very noticeable on or, preferably, above the roof. Such items might be a banner, windsock or prayer flag.

• This next solution is subtle but powerful. The **address numbers** of your home should angle upward. Visitors and guests have *chi* energy, and they find you via your address numbers. If they read those numbers at an upward slant, it lifts the first energy that finds you and helps to counteract the downward slope of your property.

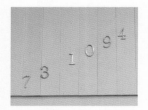

Because energy follows our gaze, when we look upward our *chi* also rises.

ENERGY RISING

• NUMBERS IN THIS FORM BRING ENERGY UP: 6 2 9
THEY ARE GOOD FOR ANY HOME. THEY ARE ESSENTIAL
IF THE PROPERTY SLOPES DOWN BEHIND THE HOUSE.

• THIS FORM IS JUST FINE IN ANY OTHER INSTANCE: 6 2 9

• THESE TWO ARE NEVER RECOMMENDED: 6 2 9   6
                                                2
                                                9

THEY BRING ENERGY DOWN BECAUSE EACH SUBSEQUENT DIGIT IS
LOWER THAN THE ONE BEFORE. IT'S EVEN MORE IMPORTANT NOT
TO USE THIS FORM IF THE PROPERTY SLOPES DOWN BEHIND THE
HOME. IT WORSENS THE PROBLEM.

• Another solution is to have a **water feature** outside the front door. Water *mauka* to a building symbolically changes the building's orientation, making it the *makai* side. The water should not be stagnant.

If the water is flowing, its direction should be toward the house: Prosperity is flowing in. It is also fine to have a fountain with water flowing in all directions, as long as some of the water is flowing toward the home.

This waterfall is auspicious because it directs water toward the main door of the house. Water symbolizes abundance, and the abundance is headed into the front door.

MORE WATER

IN HAWAIIAN, THE WORD FOR FRESH WATER IS *WAI* (OFTEN PRONOUNCED "VAI.") FRESH WATER WAS SO VALUED THAT THE WORD FOR WEALTH IS *WAIWAI*, "MORE WATER." IN CHINESE THE CHARACTER FOR WATER IS *SHUI*, USUALLY PRONOUNCED "SHWAY." THIS WORD IS ALSO A SLANG TERM FOR MONEY. WATER IS THE SOURCE OF LIFE ON EARTH. IT SYMBOLIZES ABUNDANCE IN FENG SHUI. CLEAR, MOVING WATER IS ALWAYS PREFERRED BECAUSE IT HAS MORE ENERGY, MORE *CHI*. STILL WATER THAT LOOKS STAGNANT, ESPECIALLY IF IT'S GREEN AND SCUMMY, IS WORSE THAN NO WATER. STAGNANT WATER SYMBOLIZES STAGNANT ENERGY. IF YOU USE STILL WATER, SUCH AS WITH A BIRDBATH, BE SURE TO KEEP THE WATER CLEAN AND FRESH——NO MOSQUITO BREEDING!

This is the Chinese character *shui*, meaning water. In Cantonese, it is used as slang to refer to money.

Inside
The next three solutions are within the home.

• Put a **picture of a mountain** on the back wall. The picture represents a window, and if what you see through that "window" is a mountain, a mountain is symbolically behind the home. In this instance the picture should not show water in the foreground with a mountain behind, just the mountain itself.

Sansevieria trifasciata is considered to direct energy upward because of its shape. It's a very easy plant to grow. Here it's on a pincushion plant holder in a very small vase with water. It can live that way for months, sometimes years.

• Put a **plant** with an upward form along the back wall of the house. It should be towards the center of the back wall, not towards one of the corners. One of the best plants to use in this instance is *Sansevieria trifasciata* (also called snake plant or mother-in-law's tongue.) Its rigid, pointed leaves don't splay out and point at people; they just point up and thereby conduct energy upward. It's also one of the easiest plants to grow, indoors or out.

• Another way to lift energy within the home is to hang a very tiny **wind chime** just inside the front door. Hang it from the ceiling, so when the door is opened a few inches, the wind chime lightly tinkles. The sound is above you and is high pitched, so it lifts energy. This only works on hinged front doors, not sliders. Sometimes, especially in condos, the front door reaches all the way to the ceiling. In that case, you could put a well-tuned door harp high on the inside of the door. Door harps are not common, so try looking for them at online sources, such as eBay. Never use bells that just clang against the door. They are inauspicious as well as obnoxious.

Behind the House

The final three solutions are for use at the back of the house.

• Grow **plants** with an upward form directly behind the house. Their shape counteracts the downward slope. If you don't mind tall plants, use palms or Italian cypress. When a lower plant is desired, such as on a *lānai*, use *Sansevieria trifasciata*. It does well in sun or deep shade.

• Put an image of a **turtle** behind the home. Directly behind the home is best, not toward one of the corners. In feng shui the turtle is the protective being behind a building. It should be facing away from the home, since it symbolizes an awareness of what could approach the home from behind. When the land slopes down behind a building, the turtle's energy is missing. The turtle sculpture symbolically restores that energy. The bigger the better.

• This last solution is frequently recommended: Put electric **lighting** behind the house. A spotlight on a tall pole, facing the house, is ideal—it doesn't need to be on every night, but it does need to be functioning. If a spotlight doesn't appeal to you, or it's not feasible to have one, use any form of exterior lighting, preferably directed upward—even tiny lights on a string, or solar lights. Light has an uplifting quality.

Besides being a symbol of protection in Chinese thought, the *honu* (turtle) is also a powerful *ʻaumākua*, or guardian spirit, for many people in Hawaiʻi.

Obscure
Entrance

The entrance to your home should be obvious. Good energy needs to find you. The front door area is the most important portal of energy in your life. A hidden entrance says energy is missing you—it can't find you. Don't confront *chi* energy with the question: "Where do I go?" When that energy eventually finds you, it will be somewhat weakened. Feng shui is greatly concerned with initial impressions. Because they are most memorable, they are most powerful.

If the entrance to your home is obvious, just keep it tidy and spacious feeling. Don't have too many small plants—keep it simple. Jade plant is one of the best choices to greet people outside your front door. Its leaves are rounded, so energy *rolls* in easily. Its leaves are fat, suggesting abundance. And it's easy to grow. Consider having the plant(s) in noticeable pots, such as red ones. This isn't appropriate or necessary in all homes, but sometimes it's the perfect spark to draw the eye to your door.

Opposite: This bright red pot (holding a jade plant) is outside the front door of a condo, where the rules would prevent painting the door red. The red color draws the eye (a form of *chi* energy) toward the door.

SOLUTIONS

If your front door area is not obvious, make it so. Here are tips for various situations:

• If the home is freestanding and the official front entry is on the side of the house (or worse, at the back of the house), use **signage**. "*E komo mai*" means "Welcome" or "Come In." You can have a sign that is just your last name or names, such as "The Beamers," or "The Beamer 'Ohana." Using more than one word makes the sign more noticeable, although the simple word "Welcome" gets someone headed in the right direction.

• **Painting** your front door is a simple and ideal way to make it noticeable. If you choose red—a strong choice— you might want to prime the

The front door of this home is left open most of the time for air circulation, so the screen door is painted red to be noticeable. Shoes are neatly pointed in the same direction for less chaos. The jade plant has fat, rounded leaves that symbolize abundance rolling in.

door with brown first. That way you won't have to apply as many coats of paint to get a saturated color.

• If the doorway to your condo or apartment is one of many down a hallway, try to use a very bright or noticeable **doormat**.

• If your residential complex doesn't allow doormats, you can still hang a bright **tassel** from your doorknob.

One of my clients hung a *lei* from her condo screen doorknob so I would know where to go. She used bright red artificial hibiscus, and I didn't even have to look at the address number. I was drawn right to that red *lei*.

The red tassel makes an attractive eye-catcher on an otherwise plain door.

The yellow glass knob catches light, and the red tassel is added for good measure. It's a nice color combination.

THE COLOR OF ENERGY

BOTH RED AND YELLOW ARE TRADITIONAL HAWAIIAN COLORS. THEY ARE THE MOST VISIBLE OF ALL COLORS TO THE HUMAN EYE. THEY ARE ALSO IMPORTANT COLORS IN FENG SHUI. RED IS THE MOST POWERFUL COLOR BECAUSE IT IS THE COLOR OF BLOOD——A VERY ESSENTIAL SUBSTANCE! SINCE BOTH COLORS ARE QUITE NOTICEABLE, THEY ARE GOOD CHOICES FOR MAKING YOUR FRONT DOOR MORE OBVIOUS.

• A **wind chime** hung near a front door can make it more noticeable because the wind chime moves and makes sounds. Both movement and sound are things that attract *chi* energy. Make sure the sound of the wind chime is appreciated by all in the household and any close neighbors who will hear it. Making your neighbors *huhū* (angry) is not good feng shui!

STAIRS

A ny stairs leading to your front door are very important. They guide and influence the energy that comes into your life. It is preferable that stairs leading to the front door go up. This lifts energy and suggests an optimistic life. However, upward stairs to the front door *must* have risers, which are the vertical pieces connecting the horizontal treads on which you walk. Without risers, energy slips through the gaps and doesn't reach your front door. The energy already has your name on it and is trying to find you, but it's slipping away. This symbolizes opportunities slipping away.

Top left: These stairs have treads, but no risers. You can see through the stairs to what is below. That means some *chi* energy is sliding away through the stairs and not arriving at the front door.

Top center: These steps don't have risers, but it's not a big issue in this case because they lead to a pavilion, not the main house.

Top right: Because these stairs have risers (the vertical board that connects the treads that your feet step on), *chi* energy moves up to the *lānai* and the front door.

Bottom: These worn lava stones are the front steps leading to the front courtyard. There are no missing risers, so energy can fully reach the front entry.

SOLUTIONS

• The best solution is to install **risers**.

• This isn't feasible in condos or apartments, so the next best thing is to make the front door area very obvious. Use objects that **move**, **make sounds**, are **colorful** or are otherwise very **noticeable**. Any breadwinning adults in the household should like the object(s); otherwise this will adversely affect *their* energy. A person who lives there should *like* their front door area.

• If there are restrictions in your residential complex, you can just hang a lovely **tassel** from your outside doorknob. It's certainly better than nothing.

• If the stairs go *down* toward the door, make sure the area around the outside of your front door seems bright—very bright. Potted **plants** can help with this. Especially useful are those with white variegation on the leaves, such as dwarf *laukalakoa*, also known as dwarf snowbush (*Breynia disticha*).

This plant is ideal at any doorway for several reasons: The leaves are round, not pointy. Round leaves symbolize energy rolling easily in at your door. Pointed leaves, especially if they are stiff, symbolize swords. They cause the energy to become irritated or wary: "Don't come too close," they seem to be saying. The snowbush's form is naturally compact and may never need pruning. Finally, it looks fabulous and grows well in a pot. The last thing you want is a plant that looks scrawny or sickly at your front door! Instead, it should be full and healthy.

Another nice choice would be variegated jade plant (*Crassula ovata*). These plants are good around any front door, but they are especially useful when the outside stairs to the front door go down. The white in the leaves brightens the area.

Dwarf snowbush has a naturally compact rounded form and is not invasive like the larger snowbush. It could be used to line an entrance path or flank a front door.

Slipper Clutter

Slippers are placed neatly outside the front door. This makes the area more tranquil and symbolizes accomplishing your goals.

O nce *chi* energy has found your front door, it mustn't get bogged down in clutter. Clutter symbolizes stagnation in your life. The worst place for it is at your front door. The fresh energy that is ready to enter your home should be able to do so without getting waylaid.

Very often, there are **too many slippers** outside the front door. Sometimes every shoe in the house is stored outside the front door. Find another place to put extra shoes or slippers. One or two pairs of slippers per person is plenty for the front door area. If it's a large household, keep it to one pair per person.

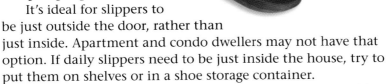

It's ideal for slippers to be just outside the door, rather than just inside. Apartment and condo dwellers may not have that option. If daily slippers need to be just inside the house, try to put them on shelves or in a shoe storage container.

Wherever slippers (or any shoes) are stored, they should be facing the same direction. They are below our feet, so they represent our foundation. If they are facing opposite directions, they symbolize our going against ourselves and not getting very far in life. It doesn't matter *which* direction the shoes are facing, as long as it's the *same* direction.

Kichitto soroe nasai means "arrange the slippers properly at the doorstep" in Japanese. This was traditionally considered important in Japan because it indicated what life was like within the house. Feng shui takes that concept a step further and believes that this arrangement helps to *affect* what happens within the house.

House
on Poles

Houses that are up on poles are common in Hawai'i and many other tropical areas. They allow for better air circulation, offer flood protection and help keep the living area free of pests, such as mosquitoes and centipedes. However, a house on poles is considered ungrounded and not well supported. Such houses may be structurally quite sound, while still having an energetic problem.

If the space below the house is enclosed, the problem is solved. The walls do not have to be solid. They can be somewhat open for air circulation. Lattice with diamond-shaped openings is not a good choice, because the angle pointing upward symbolizes fire. The house is over fire, and that's not a safe symbol.

Horizontal slat boards are generally preferable, because the horizontal plane symbolizes Earth energy and is grounding. I've seen this done where two widths of boards are used to create a pleasing pattern. If the space below the house cannot be enclosed, use small mirrors on or near the ground, facing up at the house. They are symbolically helping to support the house.

Mirrors are also useful when any part of a second story extends beyond the lower story (a cantilever.) If the upper part that extends is a *lānai*, not an

Left: Lattice with diamond-shaped openings is not as good as lattice with open horizontal boards.

Below: The small mirror is near the base of the support pole for the house. The shiny side of the mirror reflects upward and symbolically supports the house.

Opposite: A house on poles without lattice below is seen to be less supported than one with lattice.

A cantilever is an upper floor of a building protruding out over a lower floor. Even this small cantilever could use a little feng shui support.

enclosed living space, the mirrors are still helpful, but they're not essential.

Cars parked directly below a home can cause an energetic disturbance. This is most problematic if a bed is directly above a parked car. If it's a guest bed, there's no problem, but if the bed is slept in regularly, put a small mirror on the ceiling of the garage exactly above the car and facing down at it. If you don't have access to the ceiling, the mirror can go under the bed in the room upstairs, facing the floor. Alternatively, a crystal can be hung above the car, or placed under the bed. Remember, if you've placed a mirror or crystal under the bed, be careful when cleaning under there!

I'm standing on a car putting a small mirror on the ceiling of the garage.

Inset: There's the mirror I placed. It's reflecting down to keep the busy car energy from affecting the bed upstairs above it.

Blue Roof

W e've all seen them, but thankfully only a few of us have them. Blue roofs are lovely, but unfortunately feng shui strongly cautions against them. The color blue can symbolize water, like the blue ocean, and water in turn symbolizes money. When blue is the color of the roof, it symbolizes water flowing over and away from the home; that is, *money* is flowing away from you, suggesting more expense and/or less income in your life.

It doesn't matter whether it's gorgeous blue tile, a blue tin roof, or even a blue tarp on your property—don't use that color. Use *any* other color. If you've already got a blue roof and can't change it, here are some solutions; but if you have a choice, it is *much* better not to have the problem in the first place. Feng shui views it as a very serious and difficult situation.

In the same way a crystal refracts light into rainbows, it can be useful for dispersing problematic energy.

SOLUTIONS

• A clear, faceted **crystal** symbolizes dispersion in feng shui, because the crystal can disperse light into rainbows. The crystal can be natural or manufactured. Put the crystal anywhere inside the home, above head height, and it can symbolize a dispersion of the roof's energy before it affects the residents. Leaded glass crystals often have a hole in them and can be hung, or they can just be placed on a high shelf or ledge.

• One of the uses of a **mirror** in feng shui is to reflect away and push back unwanted energy. To push away the influence of the blue roof, put a mirror (any size) inside the home, facing up. The mirror should be above head height, such as on top of a ledge or soffit, or on a tall piece of furniture.

Bumpy Driveway

The road or driveway to your home should be fairly smooth. If the road is excessively bumpy, good fortune (including money) is seen as bouncing off before reaching you.

I feng shui'd for a woman who warned me in advance that the road to her home had severe potholes. She said I wouldn't need a four-wheel drive, but that it would seem as though I did. When I turned off the highway onto her road, I got a little nervous. It was a one-lane road that went directly *makai* between two rock walls. It had been paved at one time, but now there were more massive potholes than pavement. When I arrived, I explained the feng shui concern about bumpy roads leading to one's home, and tears welled up in her eyes. "The County of Hawai'i owns that road, and they told me to

my face that they have no intention of ever fixing it. They said they wished they didn't own it, and were counting on people using an entirely different road in the future."
I scratched my head for a while, but then I remembered the feng shui solution of using the color red when something is broken and can't be fixed.

A drop of red nail polish in the ruts of a bumpy road can be a symbolic solution to a troubling feng shui problem.

Red symbolizes new blood and the idea that things will be different. I suggested that she take red nail polish and walk all the way up the road, putting one drop in each pothole, and saying each time, "You're fixed now! This is the best I can do, so consider yourself fixed," or words to that effect. Well, bless her heart, she actually did it (it was a rather long road). She reported back that within a week of using the red nail polish, both she and her landlady, who lived below her, received unexpected windfalls of money.

SOLUTION

If you can make the road or driveway to your house **smooth**, then do it. That's the best solution. But if smoothing the bumps isn't feasible at the moment, try using **red**. It could be paint, nail polish, whatever, but keep the amount very small for the sake of the ʻāina. Say out loud at the time that you use it that the situation is fixed.

What you're doing is making a small physical statement that something has changed. Red is the color of blood and symbolizes a new birth—a fresh situation. Don't ever use this symbolic cure instead of fixing something where safety is an issue, though! Powerful as it is as a symbol, red can't make something safe that is physically unsafe.

Neighbor Noise

Hawai'i has a very agreeable climate. Therefore walls here are often thinner than in temperate zones. We live outside more—the *lānai* is often the most-used room. Our windows and doors are often left open for air circulation, as well. If noise is coming in along with the fresh air, that's a problem. Noise is damaging to your aura as well as to your mind.

SOLUTION

In this situation, use a **mirror** to reflect away the disturbance. The mirror should face the direction the noise is coming from. Put it on the outside of your home, if possible. If the outside is not accessible, the mirror can go in a window, directly against the glass pane. If the disturbance is coming from a neighbor below you, put the mirror on the floor, tucked under a piece of furniture. If the disturbance is from a neighbor above you, put the mirror on the ceiling, and paint the back of it the color of the ceiling. Remember, always face the shiny side toward the disturbance. You are pushing it away.

If the disturbance is truly horrible (such as a drug house) use a ***bagua* mirror**. The *bagua* mirror is a special feng shui mirror that not only pushes negative energy away but also helps to restore good order. It does this because the eight *I Ching* trigrams around the frame of the mirror are arranged in a balanced way to represent perfect order. (Check the glossary for more discussion of the *I Ching*.) Do not use a *bagua* mirror indiscriminately— don't just put one above your front door to bring in good fortune. It's a mirror—it reflects; its job is to push things away. An eight-sided mirror must have the

This is a genuine feng shui *bagua* mirror correctly oriented. Any *bagua* mirror must have the *I Ching* trigrams (lines) around the outside of the mirror. The three unbroken lines must be at the top, below the little eyehook. Those lines are *yang* and symbolize life. If this mirror were mistakenly placed upside down, it would say "house of the dead," and be appropriate (as such) for mausoleum use only.

This eight-sided mirror has no *I Ching* trigrams around the outside, so it is not a *bagua* mirror. It has no special feng shui use, other than being a mirror.

trigrams around it to be a *bagua* mirror. Otherwise, it's simply an octagonal mirror. Not that there's anything wrong with an octagonal mirror— just don't expect it to be as powerful as a *bagua*. Be aware that *bagua* mirrors are primarily for use outside the home. There are only a few rather rare instances when a *bagua* mirror is appropriate inside a home.

These are the three kinds of mirrors that I recommend most frequently for pushing energy away:

• Tiny **flat** dime-sized mirrors, from a craft-supply store. Flat mirrors reflect energy directly back toward where they are aimed (the direction of the shiny side.) One of their main advantages is that they can be found in very small sizes, so you can use them discreetly.

• **Convex** mirrors, from an auto-supply store. Convex mirrors bulge out (see Fig. A) and reflect energy from many directions. They are especially useful to push away busy highway energy. They're also good for dispersing energy so that it is not reflected directly back to its source.

• **Concave** mirrors (see Fig. B) curve inward like the inside of a bowl and are commonly used for shaving or applying makeup. In feng shui, they are used to absorb energy and are the best choice when the object whose energy is being pushed away is very close to your home and *much* larger than it, such as a skyscraper next door or a mountain smack-dab next to your entrance. Concave mirrors enlarge an image

FIG. A

FIG. B

that is a few inches away, but beyond that distance they turn the image upside down. The message you are sending out by using such a mirror is this: "You're not so big and important. I can turn you upside down."

• Ornamental silver glass balls (like large silver Christmas ornaments) can be used outside instead of mirrors.

Gazing balls of mirrored glass are often used in feng shui, both inside (to see behind you), and outside (to reflect away harsh influences).

When placing a mirror to reflect away undesirable energy, say out loud what you're doing and why you're doing it. You only have to say this once—at that moment. It makes the cure stronger, because your guardian beings then know why you're doing it. It also insures that *you* know why you're doing it—not just because "someone said to."

A note: The disturbance may not go away, but it will probably become less noticeable.

Other Noises

Lively drumming is a great workout, relieves stress and heralds fresh new energy. It's an ecological substitute for fireworks—especially near coral reef systems, which are very vulnerable to the chemicals in fireworks.

   • **Fireworks** are quite noticeable at certain times in
Hawai'i. There is a belief that only bad spirits flee from
fireworks—but the truth is, just as many, if not more, *good*
spirits are running from the sound as well. Fireworks are
very polluting, especially when set off near water. Bells and
drums do not pollute at all and do a great job of ushering in
a new vibration.

• **Coqui frog** noise is inappropriate in Hawai'i. In fact, it's inappropriate anywhere except Puerto Rico, where the frogs originated and where their natural predators have evolved. The high-pitched sound can pierce a person's aura like an arrow. Yes, it is a natural sound, but the population density these frogs have reached in Hawai'i is far greater than they naturally reach in Puerto Rico. Coqui noise here can reach 70 to 90 decibels, and noise of only 35 decibels has been proven to raise people's blood pressure significantly while they are sleeping, even if they are not awakened by it (this was reported in the *European Heart Journal*, Feb. 12, 2008). If there are coquis in your area, join your local control group to rid the Islands of this invasive pest.

• **Waves crashing** can be unsettling if they're too close and too big. If your peaceful home is disturbed by loud ocean noise, try putting a mirror outside facing the ocean. That is the best that feng shui has to offer as a solution if you're planning to stay in your house, but the classic feng shui advice is not to live quite so close to the breakers.

This *lānai* is only about 30 feet from the water's edge. Between the home and the ocean there's shrubbery just beyond the deck and an ancient *milo* tree right at the water. Without these the home would be too exposed.

"Dead End" Sign near Home

A"Dead End" sign that you pass by daily coming to or going from your home is not good for you. The word "dead" is the more problematic of the two words. We're all going to die soon enough without having it rubbed in our face continually. If someone's first language isn't English, this problem will probably affect them much less, if at all.

SOLUTIONS

The first solution is real, but is likely to be impossible to accomplish. The second solution isn't as strong, but it may well be the best you can do.

• It's a long shot, but you could see if the powers that be would **change** the sign's wording. Any of the following are harmless symbolically, and actually give more accurate information. Hopefully someday all the "Dead End" signs will be changed in Hawai'i, and the problem will vanish.
  ⊙ Not a Through Street
  ⊙ No Through Street
  ⊙ No Outlet

• If changing the sign proves impossible, **ignore** the sign as much as you can. Never refer to a "Dead End" sign when giving directions to your home. ✑

Opposite: This is a harsh way to say "Not a Through Street"

INTERIOR

The truth is that the best feng shui homes are often somewhat plain and regular looking. The old plantation-style houses are usually of very good design for making successful lives. They've got four corners, just where they should be. You never have to guess where the front door is, although once you get there, some of those (especially the plantation manager homes) do have glass-front doors.

Front Door

This mahogany front door is solid and symbolizes a well-protected home. The front area is simple, elegant and welcoming.

If there are glass panels in your front door, the glass should be primarily **translucent**, not transparent. If the glass is clear (transparent), someone could stand outside your home and look right in. Their eyesight—their visual energy—is coming into your space without being invited. That symbolizes a home where the residents are not adequately in control of the circumstances of their lives.

SOLUTIONS

• Use **frosted, etched, beveled or stained glass** to solve the problem in a very aesthetic way. If replacing the clear glass is not feasible, use sheer curtains or rice paper attached to the inside of the door, creating a screen over the glass. Light can still come in, but not intrusive vision. White fabric lining looks like rice paper but is more durable.

The window shade on the side window lets light in, yet protects the privacy of the home. To improve this tranquil scene even more, I'd suggest a table with rounded corners, since one right angle seems to be pointed at the door.

•If the front door has narrow windows beside it, they should be **screened**, just like a glass door. Alternatively, tall **plants** could be placed in front of the side windows, inside and/or out, to screen the view.

If there's a double front door, use both sides occasionally. If there's a side that's not usually used, open it at least once a month, and make sure the hinges don't squeak. Any door in the home should be able to open fully to the wall—without, of course, damaging the wall. So don't let furniture, clothes, or clutter prevent doors from opening fully. It's best not to squeeze *chi* energy as it's trying to enter. If the knobs or handles of two different doors can touch each other, they are called "clashing knobs." They represent two heads knocking against each other—disharmony and arguments. This does not apply to kitchen cabinets, just doors you can pass through.

• **Rehang** one of the doors so the knobs can't touch.

• If that's not possible, hang a red **ribbon** or red **tassel** from every knob that can touch another knob. The red represents blood and says, "There's new blood—a new dynamic is happening."

Both of these double doors should be used at least occasionally, so *chi* energy feels welcomed. These doors should also be curtained off or otherwise screened, so *unwanted* energy doesn't enter.

Back Windows

The most frequent feng shui problem I see in Hawai'i homes is the failure to retain *chi* energy. The view becomes too important, too soon. You can see right through the house the instant you step in, sometimes even before you enter. If the first thing your guests say is, "What a beautiful view you have!" that means their energy is not staying in your home for a moment. That's your clue and your challenge. You want them to say, "Your home is so nice, *and* the view is out of this world." First the home, then the view—not the other way round. Energy *must* stay in your home and circulate. Otherwise there's likely to be a subtle, nagging feeling that "life is elsewhere."

If the wall that is opposite (and visible from) the front door is an outside wall, it should not, if possible, have windows and doors you can clearly see through. It is especially important not to have a clear window or door in a direct line with the front door (see Fig. C). If the clear openings on the back wall are not in a direct line with the front door, more energy is able to stay in the house and will not escape too quickly (see Fig. D).

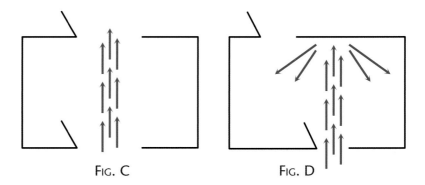

FIG. C   FIG. D

SOLUTIONS

The real solution in this case is often not acceptable to the resident, but it has my high recommendation: Keep the light, but screen the view. This, of course, horrifies most people, and their response is, "No way! We paid dearly for this view." That's understandable, but the view really shouldn't be the most important thing about the whole home. Sweeping vistas are wonderful, but it's important that they don't become so all-encompassing, so "grab-you-first-thing," that the energy of the home is depleted.

• Put a **screen**, such as a *shoji*, between the front door and the back door or windows. This is guaranteed to cause energy to meander nicely around inside instead of shooting out first thing.

• Hang sheer **curtains** over the back windows or clear glass door. Sheers don't have to look like something out of your grandmother's parlor. Many of the new sheers can enhance Island interiors.

These sheer bamboo-patterned curtains are in a bedroom. Bamboo symbolizes flexibility and durability and is very appropriate in a relationship bedroom.

• Put a **showstopper** somewhere between the front door and the back window or door. Examples of showstoppers are a large sculpture, an extravagant tropical flower arrangement or a stunning flowering plant, such as a unique orchid. The showstopper should be at least as attention getting as the view; otherwise, it won't be a good solution.

• A symbolic remedy is to put a **mirror** (any size, even tiny) near the back door or window. Don't put the mirror *on* the window glass, just near it. Use glue or double-sided tape to attach it. The mirror should face into the house, because it is symbolically reflecting *chi* back in.

This crystal is inconspicuously hung near the foyer light fixture. The front and back doors are in a direct line and the crystal symbolizes *chi* being dispersed throughout the house.

• Another symbolic remedy is to put a **cut-crystal object** between the front door and the back door or window. Some people hang a crystal from string or fishing line. It can be hung at any convenient height. Others prefer to put a cut-crystal object on a table, such as a paperweight, candlestick, vase, candy dish, bowl or decanter.

The cut crystal is symbolically dispersing *chi* energy before it vanishes out the back. If you hold the crystal object in the sunlight, it will disperse the sun's energy into rainbows. A natural crystal will also work as long as it is clear and faceted.

• A **wind chime** could also be hung between the front door and the back door or window. It is symbolically dispersing energy, because it can disperse the wind's energy into sound waves.

Excessive
Windows

W indows are good, but there can be too much of a good thing. Floor-to-ceiling windows are a problem, especially if there are a lot of them. Energy is slipping out of the house too quickly without lingering to enrich it.

SOLUTIONS

• Use **curtains** or any form of window treatment that appeals to you. Sheer curtains are excellent because they keep *chi* in a room while still allowing the light in.

• Hang a clear **crystal** in any window to help keep *chi* energy in the home. This can be done in addition to sheer curtains or by itself. Use an octagon crystal if the window receives sunlight; otherwise a disco-ball shape is always good. Crystals that sharply point down or are teardrop shaped are not appropriate. They direct energy inauspiciously downward.

Left: Slightly flattened, eight-sided clear crystals are best for making big rainbows within the home. Use them in places where the sun can reach them.

Right: Clear disco ball-shaped crystals are the most common kind in feng shui use. Their rounded shape is friendly to pass under when they are hung from the ceiling, and the facets symbolize the dispersing and breaking up of energy.

Window Treatment

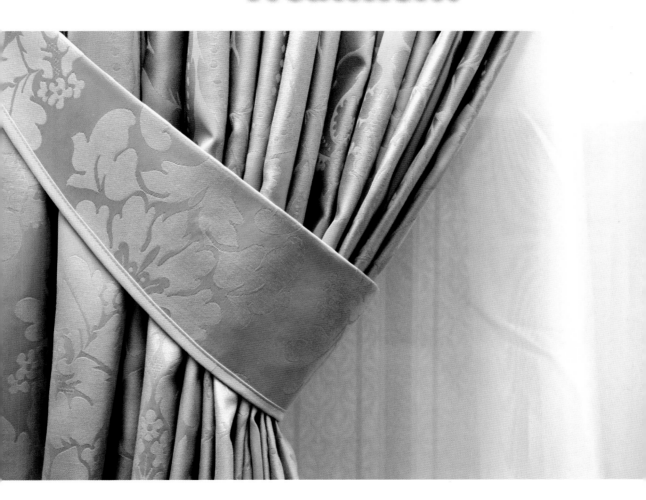

Windows can become "black holes" at night. If you draw a curtain at night, the wall continues and there is no hole for *chi* to leak out. Even during the day, certain windows in certain homes have problematic views—views in that either compromise privacy or look out at something disturbing. When curtains or shades are drawn during the day, use the kind that draw up from the bottom of the window if you only need to hide a lower view. That way you can still look out at the blue sky. Café curtains, which hang from a rod some distance below the top of the window, will also work.

These shades (called top-down bottom-up) are installed at the top but can be configured to cover only the lower part of a window. This keeps a beautiful view of palms and sky, but protects the occupants' privacy, while screening the inside from inauspicious views.

Sheer curtains provide privacy during the day, but not at night. They keep *chi* in, but if privacy is an issue at night, you'll need to have another (more opaque) layer of curtain or shade. A layered window treatment is welcome in feng shui, because it makes the home more nest-like, especially at night when that *yin* quality is most appreciated.

Split View

A split view happens anytime the energy from the door is only partially blocked, as in Fig. E. Take the width of the door (usually three feet) and extend it directly across the room. If some of the three-foot swath is blocked by a wall and some goes past it, you have a split view. This can also happen within a room, before the back wall, as in Fig. F. In this situation, the *chi* cannot escape quite so quickly as when the whole view is open, but the problem still remains; furthermore, the energy is "split" and can't comfortably circulate in the house.

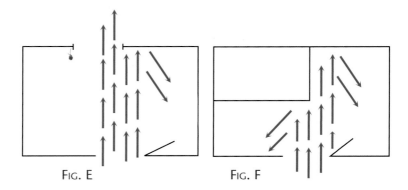

FIG. E　　　　　FIG. F

SOLUTIONS

Any of the last three solutions outlined under Back Windows are best for split views: a **hanging crystal**, a **cut-crystal** object or a **wind chime**. A mirror may also be placed on the wall that's ahead of and closest to the door, as in Fig. G and H. The other three solutions for back windows—*shoji* **screens, sheer curtains** and **show-stoppers**—are also good *in addition to*, but not in place of mirrors, crystals and/or chimes.

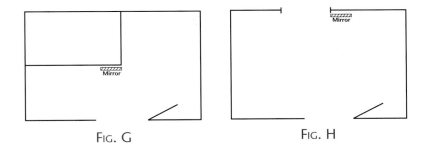

FIG. G   FIG. H

See, there's a mirror on the wall (right), hidden by the picture. The mirror symbolically enlarges the home and corrects the split view. The back wall is on the *makai* side, and so the mountain picture symbolically changes its orientation (left), the red pot's fiery color is uplifting, and the Bird of Paradise flowers point up.

Central Pole

This home has a central pole separating the living and dining areas. Central poles can symbolize obstructions in feng shui.

A pole standing near or at the middle of a room or *lānai* is a problem, because it too splits the energy. In addition to the awkwardness of walking around it, a central pole symbolizes argument, according to feng shui principles. One eye looks to one side and the other eye looks to the other, as though they were disagreeing: "This is my opinion." "Oh, no, I see things differently." Poles along the edge of a porch or *lānai* are not a problem, only central poles that you must walk around. This situation can arise when rooms are added on, and it also occurs in condos as a column rising from a counter or short wall. If something feels like a central pole, it probably is one.

The solution is to put a tall object next to the pole. That makes the pole less noticeable—it's just another tree in the forest. Here the owner used a large artificial palm.

SOLUTIONS

• Put something tall next to the pole. This makes the pole part of a grouping and starts to visually erase it. The pole is made less important, and therefore it is less of a problem. Examples of tall objects to go beside the post:

⊙ **Tall screens**, such as *shoji* screens.

⊙ **Tall plants** (real or artificial), such as rhapis, also known as lady palm, which can tolerate low-light situations better than most palms.

A tall screen can hide a central post or distract the eye from it.

It's also a space-saver within the room, because its fronds don't spread out widely from the trunk.

This rhapis palm is flanked by peace lilies. The palm is tall but doesn't reach the ceiling. Plants that touch the ceiling say you've reached your limit.

Diffenbachia, which is fairly well known by that name, though it is sometimes also called dumb cane, is another good choice. Panax works well, but only if there is enough light for it. Parsley panax *(Polyscias scuttelaria)* has delightful fernlike leaves.

⊙ **Climbing plants**, like philodendron, pothos, or hoya. These can save floor space when they are hung next to the pole and climb down it, helping to disguise it or soften its outlines somewhat. A variety of hoya that has fragrant flowers, such as *Hoya carnosa*, is especially nice.

⊙ **Tall furniture** such as bookcases, cabinets or armoires. Make sure, however, to secure the furniture in case of earthquake or *keiki*-climbing. Having unsecured, unstable tall furniture anywhere in your home is bad news, the more so if it's not against a wall. We live in Hawai'i; we have earthquakes. Part of you is a bit on edge, if only subconsciously, if you are perceiving a possible danger you haven't addressed. If you go ahead and secure things that might topple, you'll rest easier.

• You can also put a **solid mirror** on each side of the pole. This will only work if the pole is square and has flat sides. Don't use mirror tile, which chops up a person's image—it's like *karate* chops to your aura. If you use this solution, the mirrors on each side of the post must be one piece, so they will be long and rectangular. Each mirror must completely cover its side of the pole.

Whirlwind

Whirlwind energy is also called racetrack energy. It happens when *chi* energy, or people, can go in a circle through several doorways inside the home (see Fig. I). It symbolizes wasting time and getting nowhere.

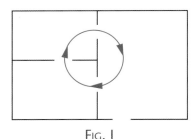

FIG. I

SOLUTIONS

• **Close a door**, at least one of the doors. This is an easy and excellent solution.

A bead curtain keeps energy from whirling around while still providing access to where you need to go.

• If there are no closable doors in the doorways, consider hanging a **beaded curtain** (or any curtain) in one of the doorways.

• Hang a **crystal** or **wind chime** in one of the doorways or anywhere above your head if you were walking in the circle through the doorways.

• A thick **rug** is a great way to slow *chi* energy, especially in Hawai'i where we are usually barefoot indoors. The feet appreciate the soft plush rug and want to linger.

"Brick Wall"

A "brick wall" is almost never made of bricks. It's just a regular interior wall that's directly in front of you as you walk into a room, a few feet away from the door. It causes you to have to turn left or right, just as soon as you've entered. It represents an obstacle—however, it is easily fixed with symbolic remedies, so no need to take out walls!

SOLUTIONS

• Hang a **picture** with depth and perspective on the "brick wall" that draws you into the scene.

• Install a faux **painting** or **wall mural** (many are available on the Internet now) that likewise draws you into the scene. You're trying to make the wall visually vanish.

• Put a **mirror** on the "brick wall" facing the door. The mirror opens up and expands the space. However, a large mirror feels jarring to me in this location, as if I'm being reflected back out of the house, so I usually recommend putting a small mirror behind a picture with depth.

As soon as you step in, you have to turn left to go on into the home. The wall just inside the front door is called a "brick wall"—even though it's wood. It can symbolize obstacles and thwarted plans. The ideal picture on this kind of wall would have more depth and perspective than this *ti* picture.

(Inset): Behind the *ti* picture is a little mirror to symbolically open up the wall. When a *large* mirror is placed on the "brick wall" it opens up the wall, but can also push energy back out of the home too quickly.

Ceiling

The three most common ceiling problems encountered in Hawai'i are exposed beams, sloping ceilings and fans. Most local rooms are fairly well proportioned, but sometimes the ceilings are too high or low.

A person shouldn't spend a lot of time directly under an exposed beam. The beam is supporting the pressure of the roof, and the area directly below it, all the way to the floor, has a harsh, pressurized energy. Being directly under beams only occasionally is not a problem, but definitely don't have your bed under a beam. People spend a third of their lives in bed, so the area in which it's situated really affects a person. Don't put important seating right under an exposed beam, either—not your desk chair, not your dining chair, and not your favorite lounge chair. When you're standing at the stove, a beam should not be directly above you.

SOLUTIONS

If an open beam is directly above you in any of those five locations, here's what to do:

• **Cover** the beam. This is the best solution, because then the problem goes away as far as feng shui is concerned. If putting up a new ceiling is not feasible, consider stapling fabric or *lauhala* matting (woven from *hala* leaves) over the beams.

Lauhala matting not only visually erases troubling beams; it has a nice tropical feel to it and can be found in many craft or hula-supply stores.

I went to a client's home in Volcano, and directly over his bed was the place where about seven big beams came together. I explained the problem and suggested a quick fix of pinning up fabric over the beams. He located a prayer shawl from India that he liked a lot. We went ahead and pinned it up. (There's a lot more power in fixing a feng shui problem immediately than in procrastinating.) He called me the next morning to say that for the last five years he'd had edema in his ankles when he first woke up. This was the first time in five years that his ankles weren't swollen!

• **Paint** the beams the same color as the ceiling. They are less noticeable then, and thus less of a problem.

When an open beam is painted the same color as the ceiling, it blends in more and is less of a problem.

• Hang a **crystal** from the beam. The crystal is a symbol of energy dispersal, and it suggests that the harsh energy is dispersed harmlessly into the air before it reaches you. The crystal should be clear and faceted, and it should be hung directly above the area where the person will be lying, sitting or standing. Any height is fine. It can be hung with clear monofilament, such as fishing line. A **wind chime** also symbolizes dispersed energy and may be used instead of the crystal.

This wall sconce directs *chi* upwards, working against the pressurized feeling of an exposed beam.

• Put an upward-pointing **light** directly below the beam. Because the energy of the light shines up, it counteracts the beam's downward energy. Examples of "uplights" are torchières, wall sconces and spotlights that shine up.

• Put an object or plant that has an **upward-pointed shape** directly below the beam. *Sansevieria* is a good choice.

• If none of the above are feasible, then put a small **mirror** (such as a mirror coaster) on a table directly under the beam. The mirror reflects upward and symbolically pushes away the energy of the beam.

• Bamboo flutes are often recommended by some feng shui consultants as a solution for beams. I personally think they can look odd with some décors, but if you like the look, they are helpful. If you choose to use flutes, hang two on each problem beam. Each flute should be fairly close to the wall and hung at a 45-degree angle, with the mouthpiece pointing down. Usually red ribbon or cord is used to hang them. The symbol is that the uplifting notes of the flute and the air passing through the bamboo help to raise the energy of the beam.

There are two instances when exposed beams are not a problem. One is where the roof is held up by an open framing of many two-by-fours. This is the case in some of the old plantation houses. No one beam is holding up much weight, except the center beam running down the middle, and that's the only one to be concerned about.

The other instance is where the beams are extremely high above you—say, 30 feet. In that case, their negative influence is diluted by all the space between you and them.

Slanted Ceiling

A slanted ceiling (even if the beams are hidden) presents another feng shui problem. The energy under the high part of the ceiling is more expansive, and the energy under the low part is more pressurized. If the lowest part of the ceiling is less than eight feet above the floor, try not to put the head of a bed there. Also try to avoid putting much-used seating under the low part of a slant.

If moving the furniture is not an option, use these three solutions listed above: **lights**, **mirrors** or **up-pointing objects**. You can also suspend a **crystal** from the highest part of the ceiling, as in Fig. J, letting it hang so it's level with the lowest part. That symbolically creates a level ceiling.

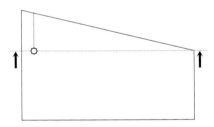

Ceiling fans

Ceiling fans are common in Hawai'i, and are especially welcome where cross-ventilation is absent. Despite their usefulness, they can bring some harsh energy into a room. The most noticeable part of the fan is called a "blade." That word suggests a cutting energy, just like a knife blade—and in fact, you certainly wouldn't want to put your finger in the way of a moving fan blade. The other problem with ceiling fans is that the blades are spread out like a hand's splayed fingers, so the fan symbolizes a "hand" over you, pushing down. That "hand" pressurizes the energetic space directly under the fan, just as an exposed beam does.

The teardrop-shaped fan pull (left) is lovely but doesn't have any special feng shui use because there are no facets in the glass. The disco ball-shaped fan pull (right) can easily clip onto an existing fan. Even though it is pressed glass, it still represents dispersion because it is faceted.

Below Left: These woven fan blades are especially appropriate for low ceilings becuse they are light colored and have less presence in the room.

Center: These fan blades are some of the friendliest I've ever seen. They remind me of a fan an aunty would use to cool herself.

Right: These fan blades are so gentle looking that they hardly deserve the name "blade." They circulate air quite well and are energetically friendly.

SOLUTIONS

Luckily, there are several easy solutions, so you won't have to get rid of your nice ceiling fan.

• The easiest solution is to use a **crystal fan pull** from a hardware store. Even the pressed-glass ones that look like crystals are fine. The little crystal fan pull does its job well. It hangs between the fan and you and symbolizes the dispersion of the harsh energy before it reaches you.

• If the fan blades are the **same color** as the ceiling, they aren't as noticeable. So they aren't attracting as much *chi* energy and are less of a problem. Often the blades can be flipped over to show a white side. If not, try painting them white or whatever color the ceiling is.

• There are some new fan blades in certain stores that are not a feng shui problem. Fan blades that look like *lauhala* or woven coconut fronds have a friendly energy, like an aunty fanning herself in church. Don't get the open-weave rattan type, though; they won't move air around.

Ceiling Height

It's usually obvious when a ceiling is **too low**. The space feels cramped. Ceilings can also be **too high**, in which case they don't contain energy well. It's difficult to feel settled in such homes. Very high ceilings are more suited for businesses than homes.

SOLUTIONS FOR LOW CEILINGS

• **Paint** them white so they feel more expansive.

• Use **uplights**—lights that shine upward. They lift the oppressive energy.

SOLUTIONS FOR HIGH CEILINGS

• **Paint** them a bit darker than usual to make them seem lower.

• Install **crown molding** around the walls some distance below the ceiling. Paint the wall above the molding the same color as the ceiling.

• Most of the **light** should be directed downward. Pools of light on the floor will make it cozier.

• The **furniture** should be dark, substantial and heavy-looking to ground energy.

Skylights

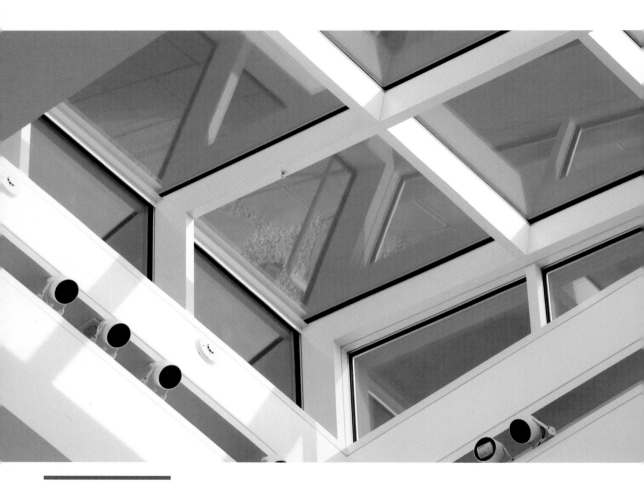

Square skylights are better than the inauspicious round "bullet-hole" type.

Skylights are fine for a home unless they are directly over the bed, stove or desk. These positions symbolize the *chi* below the skylight leaking up and out of the home. The *chi* at these three important areas should be undisturbed, not vanishing up and out.

One of the best places for a skylight is at the entrance. The area just inside and just outside the front door is called the "bright hall" (*ming tang*). The brightness of skylights uplifts the *chi* that enters your life.

Skylights are most appreciated in spaces that otherwise might have no natural light, such as long halls, or bathrooms without side windows. The "sun tube" kind of skylight is better than nothing, but it isn't the preferred kind. The reason for this caution is that the round hole can symbolize a bullet hole through the top of the house. If you have sun tube skylights, definitely use the crystal remedy below. Otherwise, it's only necessary to use one of these solutions if you have a skylight over the bed, stove or desk. But if you like the crystal solution, I recommend it to enhance any skylight.

This skylight lets welcome sunlight in, and its position above the hall—not an energetically concentrated area—ensures that it's not allowing *chi* to leak out.

SOLUTIONS

• Hang an octagonal or disco ball-shaped **crystal** in the center of the skylight. Use a clear crystal and clear monofilament, such as fishing line. Stretch a line bisecting the skylight. From the middle of that line, hang the crystal—or more than one, if you like them, on another line. They should be cleaned regularly: Isopropyl alcohol (common rubbing alcohol) is ideal. It dries quickly and leaves them sparkling. The crystal symbolizes energy dispersion.

• Hang plain white **sheer fabric** under the skylight. The sheer fabric lets plenty of light in but also keeps the *chi* from escaping upward. If the skylight is over a bed, use

Sheer fabric is useful for many feng shui solutions, containing *chi* while allowing light to pass through.

heavier fabric, if that's to your taste. The area around a bed should feel cozy and nest-like. A canopy bed is a good option under a skylight. Don't ever use this remedy over a stove, though. Never hang anything combustible over a stove.

• If the skylight has a **shade** or other form of covering, close it when sleeping in the bed, cooking at the stove or working at the desk.

Bathrooms

F eng shui considers bathrooms to be very unbalanced rooms, because they are all about water. Kitchens have water in them, too, but they are more balanced because they also have fire, as in stoves, ovens and other electrical appliances. On the *yin/yang* scale, the bathroom is much too *yin*. An easy way to balance the *yin/yang* energy of a bathroom is by keeping the decor simple. Fussy, busy decorating with a lot of little objects is *yin*. Simple, minimalist decorating is *yang*. So the simpler you keep the bathroom the better, without being clinically stark.

But matters can get worse—if the bathroom doesn't get good air circulation, it can get moldy and mildewy. In a sense, part of the home is rotting and dying. That's bound to affect your life—and not in a good way. The best bathrooms are the freshest, and that means fresh air—not air freshener in a can. What keeps a bathroom freshest is an open window to the outside. There's plenty of breeze in Hawai'i, so if there's a window, use it.

However, it's best not to use the door for bathroom air circulation. Try to keep the bathroom door closed as much as possible. That keeps the wet, *yin*, body-waste energy of that room from influencing the rest of the home. If the bathroom door is the only source of air circulation, by all means leave it open, but no more than is necessary. Perhaps enough air can get in if the door is open just a few inches. If you are considering a ceiling fan to remove moist air in the bathroom, be aware there are some extremely quiet ones on the market now.

Bathrooms that don't have a door are not a feng shui favorite. Some people consider the openness of an *en suite* bathroom a luxury, but dollars don't always equal sense. It's common sense for a bathroom to have a door, according to feng shui. It gives the user privacy and keeps the body-waste vibration confined to one area. At least use a screen or curtain to close the bathroom energy away from the adjacent room. Louver doors with openings between the slats are also not appropriate between bathrooms and other rooms, though they are fine to have as closet doors within a bathroom. I personally prefer bathroom doors with self-closing hinges. They are a cheap and easy way to take the bother out of always

Sparse decorating is *yang* and helps to balance the wet, *yin* energy of bathrooms. However, this one is too stark (easy to clean though). I could see a picture of yellow hibiscus on the wall, maybe with a blue frame or matte around it.

closing a bathroom door. There are many door-closing devices at hardware stores.

Another problem with bathrooms is the number of drains—at least three. Water is wealth, *waiwai*, so where it leaves your home is a problem area. It's best not to see the actual drain hole: If you don't see it, it's as though it's not there. Use your creativity to find ways to cover drain holes. Often it's as easy as pulling the little handle to make the stopper go down. Tub drains can be hidden by pulling the shower curtain closed. The toilet drain hole is the easiest one to hide, because all you have to do is close the lid. There are now toilet lids with self-closing hinges.

There are many kinds of self-closing hinges. This one looks like an ordinary hinge, only thicker.

There's another reason the toilet lid should be closed when the toilet is not in use, just as the bathroom door should be closed when someone is not coming or going. Lid down, then flush—it's a good habit for yourself and your children, because the lid stops the body-waste vibration from reaching you. A major feng shui problem ceases to exist with the flick of a finger. Business bathroom toilets that have only seats and no lids need to be fitted with lids.

No, this lid is not going to slam down. It gently closes itself with a slight touch of the finger—handy and hygienic.

Finally, leaky faucets need to be fixed—that's your *waiwai* leaking away.

Bathroom Décor

Because the bathroom is all about water, it is not appropriate to add decorative objects that symbolize water. I've seen Hawai'i bathrooms that seem like they are in the ocean—fish on the shower curtain, soap in a seashell and surf pictures on the wall. That's too much water for a room that's already *yin*. Plant imagery is the best decorative motif for bathrooms. Plants suck up water, so they add balance to the room. Real orchids are ideal for bathrooms, and there are some great artificial ones that are also appropriate. Bamboo is a common

design motif that works well in Asian and Indonesian décors. Pictures of flowers such as plumeria and hibiscus add a local touch, and it's easy to find nice ones. Green is a good color in bathrooms, because it symbolizes plants.

Living plants are excellent in bathrooms, especially if they don't hang down. One spiky plant that is very useful around drains is *Sansevieria trifasciata*. This species has leaves that only aim up, not out, like agave or yucca. Because the leaves of *Sansevieria trifasciata* only point up, they don't aim at people. A sharp object is placed with great care in feng shui—it mustn't point at people. The plants' upward form also counteracts the downward energy of the drain. Drains are always a problem in feng shui because they are where water (which equals wealth) exits your house. They symbolize money draining away.

Above: The leaves of *Sansevieria trifasciata* point up and help counteract the drain-down energy of the toilet.

Right: The smooth rounded rock (*pohaku*) represents stillness. It anchors your good fortune while flushes come and go. The bigger the rock, the better.

Another natural object that counteracts a "drain-away" vibration is a big, rounded, heavy rock, or *pohaku*. I recommend putting them on the floor under any sink or toilet tank. Rocks represent stillness, and the heavier the rock the better. Rounded rocks (such as water-worn ones) are easier to clean and generally look better indoors than rough rocks. Protect nice tile floors by putting felt on the rock's bottom.

And again, simple and spare is the look that's most useful in bathrooms. It can be quite elegant, just not busy or complicated. Generally, avoid patterned fabric in a bathroom. Do "statement" decorating, where the one or two decorative touches are unique and noticeable. Since bathrooms are overly *yin* because of all the water, a minimalist style brings a *yang* balance.

Center Bathroom

Any bathroom that's entirely surrounded by other living spaces is considered to be a center bathroom, whether or not it is in the actual physical center of the building. See Fig. K. In a condo or an apartment, as long as one of the bathroom walls is tangent to a space that is not in your unit, it's not a center bathroom. See Fig. L. If one of the bathroom walls is tangent to a garage, but not to an outside wall, there's no problem *if* that garage usually has a car parked in it. The energy of the car coming and going affiliates a garage with the outside. If the garage does not usually have a car parked in it, the bathroom should probably be counted as a center bathroom.

I can't think of anything worse than a center bathroom. I've known the history of several families whose homes had center bathrooms—disease, divorce, bankruptcy. Feng shui says the core of the house represents the core of your life—the things that are most vital. To put the most problematic room in that area is a recipe for trouble.

For most of humanity's history, bathrooms have been outbuildings. That's how I was raised, and it's still that way in much of the world. Modern plumbing allows bathrooms to be anywhere in the house. Most homes don't have a completely interior bathroom, although they are becoming a bit more common, especially as powder rooms in larger homes. If the bathroom has a separate water closet (toilet room) with a closeable door, that in itself is not a problem. The water closet is part of the rest of the bathroom, and if any wall of the whole bathroom is tangent to an outside wall, it is okay. A center bathroom with a skylight is still considered a center bathroom. Skylights, especially if they open, improve any bathroom, but they don't change its location.

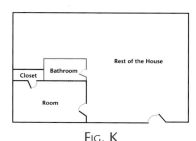

FIG. K

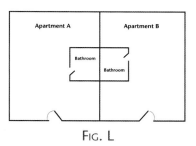

FIG. L

Fig. K: A center bathroom does not have to be in the center of the building. It only needs to be surrounded by the interior of the home on all sides.

Fig. L: These are not center bathrooms, because they touch a wall that on the other side is not in their unit.

SOLUTIONS

The only real solution is to remove the bathroom. That's out of the question for most folks, but it really does solve the problem 100 percent. Symbolic solutions can never quite achieve that. No matter what the symbolic solution, I sincerely doubt that a home with a center bathroom will ever truly support a person in achieving their greatest potential.

Except for the first two, all these remedies greatly improve the vibration of *any* bathroom. The first three remedies are specific for center bathrooms.

Mylar or reflective film isn't just for balloons! It's an easier and more flexible solution than covering all of a center bathroom's walls with mirrors.

• Mirror all the walls (including the ceiling) in the bathroom, 100 percent. I know that sounds like an extreme solution, but feng shui considers this to be a very serious situation. Preferably, the mirrors should be in rather large sheets, rather than many mirror tiles. The seams between two adjacent mirror pieces break up a person's image in an unhealthy way. We don't really look like that. Try to have as few seams as possible if you opt for this remedy. This remedy is almost never acceptable to the resident. It can be approximated by hanging more mirrors in the center bathroom.

• Another more acceptable alternative might be to cover all the walls in the bathroom with **Mylar** (shiny side facing the bathroom). Once the Mylar is in place, feel free to wallpaper or paint right over it. The reflective film is acting as a sealing agent, keeping the bathroom vibrations in that one room. Covering the Mylar will not affect the symbolic sealing of the room.

• If there is any other bathroom, **use the center bathroom less.**

• Hang a ***bagua* mirror** on the outside of the bathroom above the door. *Bagua* mirrors aren't generally used inside a home, but this is one situation where they are acceptable.

• All bathrooms benefit from having a **mirror** placed on the wall outside the door. They reflect *chi* energy away from the bathroom, even when the door is open.

• If possible, put a large **dressing mirror** on the outside of the actual bathroom door. This is occasionally done with sliding doors, although it's much more practical with hinged doors. When someone walks by that bathroom, they look through a "window" (the large mirror) and don't see a bathroom. Instead, they see more of whatever room they are already in. You are visually erasing the bathroom. This is one of the best things to do if you have a bathroom that opens directly into a kitchen. Then keep that door closed!

• Hang a very tiny (about two-inch) **wind chime** inside the bathroom, from the ceiling. I use a clear pushpin and clear filament. Hang it about six inches from the door, just low enough so that the top of the door barely touches the very bottom of the wind chime as the door is opened. The sound should be quite mild but pleasing. The reason this symbolic solution works is because as soon as the door is opened, the first sound you hear is *above you* and *high-pitched*. The drain-down vibration of the room is immediately countered because the very first sound is up. Because the sound is *high*-pitched, not *low*-pitched, it works even better. If the wind chimes are very tiny, I recommend them for absolutely any bathroom. This solution, of course, does not work with pocket doors. This is the same solution that is used to raise the energy of a home with a *mauka*-facing front door.

• Images of **animals** or **people** are also good. Animals symbolically have the "fire of life" and help to balance the water element. However, avoid water animals—fish, dolphins, whales, crustaceans or coral. Those images make a wet room wetter.

• Put **red string, ribbon** or **tape** around the sink drainpipe. Don't put it around the incoming water pipes, just the drain. You are symbolically cutting off the drain so it's not a drain anymore. This can also be done on kitchen sink drains, and if you have access under the floor, you can also do it for shower, tub and toilet drains.

Toilet

The direction a toilet is pointing is important. The energy of a toilet is considered to extend directly above it, directly below it, in front of it and behind it. The energy doesn't move side-to-side. A toilet should not be "aimed" at a bed, desk or stove, or at seating that is much used, such as a favorite lounge chair. It should also not be aimed at the front door.

Fig. M: Looking down onto a toilet, energy goes directly forward and back, through walls. In a one-story house these are the only directions to be concerned with.

Fig. N: Looking at the side of a toilet, energy goes forward, backward, up and down.

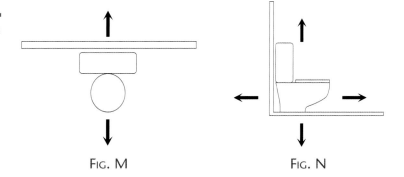

FIG. M   FIG. N

• If the back of the toilet is pointed at any of those things, put a small mirror on the wall behind the toilet tank, facing the toilet. It is symbolically keeping the vibrations of the toilet from going through to the next room. If that's a roommate's toilet and you don't have access to it, you can put the mirror in your room facing the wall with the toilet on the other side of it. When a toilet is on one side of a wall and the other side of that wall is the walkway to your front door, opportunities are symbolically being flushed before they reach your door, so definitely put up the little mirror behind the tank facing the tank.

• If the front of the toilet is pointed at any of the important things listed above, again put a small mirror at the level of the toilet, on the wall that the toilet faces. Place it so it faces the toilet and reflects it back. You can paint over the mirror if you don't want it seen. You can also put the mirror in the next room (at the same level as the toilet), but remember to keep the reflective side of the mirror facing toward the toilet, which means that the shiny side is against the wall in the next room.

• If the toilet is below a desk, bed, stove or much-used seating, put a mirror on the ceiling of the bathroom, directly above the toilet and facing the toilet. You could also put the mirror directly under the bed, desk, chair or stove, with the shiny side facing down toward the toilet.

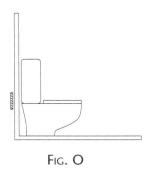

FIG. O

Fig. O: This mirror (with the shiny side toward the wall) is reflecting toilet energy away from the adjacent room.

• If the toilet is above any of those four things, put a mirror on the ceiling above the bed, desk, chair or stove, with the shiny side facing up toward the toilet. You can paint over the back of the mirror.

• For any bathroom, affix a small mirror (less than one inch in diameter) to the bathroom ceiling directly over the toilet, reflecting down onto the toilet. Glue or double-sided tape can be used to hold it. A small mirror in this location symbolizes containment of the flush-away energy of the toilet itself. Since the mirror is *above* the toilet, it *seals* it like the lid of a container. This remedy should not be used in a business bathroom, because it could make someone wonder whether they were being watched.

Foyer Stairs

I nterior upward stairs in a direct line with the front door and facing it are a major feng shui problem. Some of feng shui's greatest masters consider this to be the *most dire condition within a home.* Fortunately they're not as common in Hawai'i as on the mainland, but wherever they occur, a big problem is created. Think of it this way: *chi* comes rushing in the door, all happy and nice, dashes up the stairs, gets tired after a few steps and rolls back out the door, not to be seen again. If the stairs are very close to the door, the problem is at its most severe, representing false starts and unmet expectations.

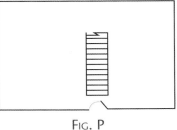

FIG. P

SOLUTIONS

• The only real solution is to redirect the bottom few stairs, with a landing and a right-angle turn, so they don't face the door (see Fig. Q). This is by far the best solution, but it is frequently not an option, especially in smaller homes.

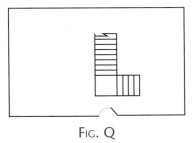

FIG. Q

• A **container** (basket or umbrella stand) near the door will symbolically catch the energy. The container must not be completely full—in fact, it can be empty.

• An inside **mirror**, above or next to the door, and on the same wall as the door, reflects the energy back into the house. Once I even used a tiny piece of glitter as the mirror, when there was no other acceptable option. The ideal mirror to use in this instance is a *bagua* mirror. They are not usually for use indoors, but this is an exception.

Opposite: These graceful-looking stairs are actually one of the most serious feng shui challenges, causing energy to roll out of the door without fully entering the house.

• A **crystal** (or even a **wind chime**) hung between the stairs and the door disperses the energy.

No Foyer

Homes without a foyer are a bit less gracious to *chi* energy than those that have one. The energy doesn't have time to catch its breath, pool up and then gently meander through the house. Without a foyer, you're just instantly in the house. Small condos and apartments, and occasionally small houses, are sometimes configured so that as soon as you step inside the front door, there's a close wall on one side and a close refrigerator on the other side. Therein lies your challenge.

SOLUTIONS

• Use a ***very* large mirror** on the side wall to enlarge it visually. This is often the most doable of solutions, and it really does the trick. The space instantly feels bigger.

• Make an area just inside the front door that **feels like a foyer.** Use different flooring there, even just a rug, but make sure it can't slip. That would suggest an unsteady foundation.

• Put an object near the door that is commonly found in foyers, and it will suggest a foyer:
- ☉ Hat or coat rack
- ☉ Mirror on the wall above a half-round table directly below it
- ☉ Straight-backed chair
- ☉ Umbrella stand

Yin and *Yang* Rooms

Rooms with an active purpose (such as a living room or office) are best in the front part of the house. They benefit from the busy *yang* energy of the road. Rooms with a quiet purpose, such as bedrooms, benefit from the restful *yin* energy toward the back of the house. It's also good not to have bedrooms directly above or behind a garage. The busy influence of the car is inappropriately close. In a larger home or an "empty nest" there can be rooms that are rarely entered, except for overnight guests. Those kinds of rooms are way too *yin*—practically stagnant.

SOLUTIONS

• If bedrooms are close to a road or other busy influence, put a **mirror** (preferably outside) facing the disturbance. The mirror can be very small, less than an inch. It is best to use a *convex* mirror if the disturbance is a *road*. The bulge of the mirror pushes back the cars in many directions.

• Use plenty of **fabric**, such as heavy curtains, and a more layered window treatment in any room that needs to be more restful. Use quiet colors.

• If active rooms are in the rear of the house, use lighter, more open furniture and at least a touch of **bright color**. Use less fabric.

• If the cars in a garage point directly at a wall that is tangent to a bedroom, put a small **mirror** in the garage. The mirror should be at headlight level, with the reflective side facing the car. The mirror reflects and symbolically pushes the car away.

• If the bedroom is over a garage, put a **mirror** (any size) on the ceiling of the garage, with the reflective side facing the car. Place the mirror either directly over the

Below: Layered window treatment is ideal in bedrooms where the softness of the extra fabric supports the quiet, *yin* activity of sleep. The drapes puddle on the floor and gently move energy upward. The decorative bamboo poles are contained in a basket so energy doesn't go down and out.

automobile or directly under the bed. Occasionally the ceiling of a garage is not a good option for a mirror. Then put the mirror in the bedroom under the bed, reflective side down.

• You can also hang a **crystal** on the ceiling of the garage above the car or cars. The crystal disperses the busy energy of the car before it reaches the quiet bedroom.

• Try livening up an unused room with **light** or **sound**. Low-wattage kinetic lighting (light that moves) can be put on a timer so that it comes on for a few hours every evening. Remember—leave the door open. For sound, leave a window open and hang a wind chime next to it. Or keep a bubbly-sounding fountain going in that room during hours when people are home.

A hammock is an irresistible way to rest or read. When putting it away, twist it, to keep it from tangling.

HOME GETAWAY

ROOMS THAT ARE RARELY USED BENEFIT FROM PEOPLE COMING AND GOING. SO LEAVE THE DOOR OPEN TO INVITE PEOPLE IN, AND GIVE YOURSELF (OR OTHER FAMILY MEMBERS) A GOOD REASON TO GO IN THERE. PERHAPS PUT THE MOST COMFORTABLE CHAIR IN THE HOUSE IN THAT ROOM. IF THERE'S ROOM (AND SUPPORT) TO HANG A HAMMOCK, THEN YOU'VE CREATED A VACATION DESTINATION IN YOUR OWN HOME. A HAMMOCK CAN BE EASILY PUT AWAY BY HANGING BOTH ENDS FROM THE SAME HOOK. I DON'T RECOMMEND HAMMOCK WITH STRETCHER BARS, BECAUSE THEY ARE PRONE TO TIPPING OVER.

Great Rooms

Great rooms are the norm for newer homes in Hawai'i. Alas, they're not a feng shui favorite. They can't ruin your life, but great rooms are just not ideal. Ideal are rooms *that feel like rooms* for distinctly different purposes. The dining room should feel like a dining room, not a TV-watching room. Quite a few times I've had clients stand inside their great room and say, "I don't know what to call this room."

SOLUTION

Use **tall furniture, screens** or **tall plants** to define areas of different use. It's not hard to give this a try. I predict you will appreciate the results in your life. 🐍

A stair *tansu* gracefully divides the quiet *punee* from the busy coming and goings near the front door. The unique shape of the *tansu* allows both privacy and a sense of openness at the same time—a nice accomplishment for a piece of furniture.

FURNITURE AND APPLIANCES

One reason that feng shui has been used for several thousand years and is still popular today is that it answers everyone's basic furniture question: "Where do I put it?" The simple answer has remained the same: put it where you can see the door and where you don't have sharp things pointing at you.

Furniture
Placement

See the Door

The first rule for furniture placement is the simplest of feng shui rules: Be able to see the door when you're using the furniture. The door is the gateway to the room, and it represents the future because it's where new things enter the room. A powerful position is one where you can easily see the doorway from the bed or chair. A weak position is one where your back is toward the door. If the furniture cannot be repositioned, use a mirror to show the doorway (Fig. R). If there's more than one door in a room, the door that's closest to the front door is usually the main door to be concerned about.

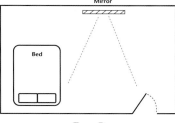

FIG. R

Your desk (at home and at work) should be positioned so you can easily see the direction of the door, at least through the corner of your eye. If you can't move the furniture, use a convex mirror, like the kind that stick on cars' outside rear view mirrors. Position it next to the computer screen if the computer is used a lot. If there are study desks in children's rooms, make sure they can see toward the door.

Beds

The bed is the most important piece of furniture in anyone's life—because we spend the most time there. Any place we spend a lot of time is important. The head of the bed should be against a solid wall, if at all possible. Some feng shui authors recommend angling the head of a bed in the corner of the room. Not me—I think it wastes space (which is fine in a large bedroom but a problem otherwise), and it creates a stagnant area where no one goes, in the corner. A child's bed can go against walls on two sides if they like that cozy feeling or if the room is small, but it's best that adults have at least 18 inches on each side of the bed. This is especially important in relationship beds. Beds (and usually desks) have whirlwind energy going around them if they are in the middle of a room and no part of the furniture touches a wall.

It is a feng shui principle that every bed needs a headboard. If nothing else, breadwinners definitely need headboards attached to their beds. A solid headboard is always best, because it represents solid backing in life. A solid headboard is especially important if there is a window directly at the head of the bed. If spouses sleep in the same bed, the solid headboard helps to reinforce the unity of their relationship. An open headboard can signify an open relationship.

Open headboards are fine for guest beds, but even *keiki* beds should have solid headboards if possible.

Futon couches are fine for guests, but not for the head of the house. They have a temporary feel and lack a good headboard. Incidentally, chairs with openings in the back are also fine for occasional seating, but a solid backing is much better for chairs that are used on a regular basis.

Above left: An open headboard is not preferred in feng shui—especially when placed directly below a window.

Above right: This headboard is lovely, but it's not recommended because of the open spaces between the bamboo poles. However, it's fine for a guest bed because no one stays there long enough to be adversely affected.

HEADBOARD ALTERNATIVES

IF IT SEEMS THAT A SOLID HEADBOARD IS NOT OBTAINABLE IN THE IMMEDIATE FUTURE, YOU CAN APPROXIMATE A HEADBOARD BY PINNING UP ONE OF THE FOLLOWING:

- *LAUHALA*

- A BEACH MAT, BUT NOT THE KIND THAT FOLDS UP IN THIRDS

- FABRIC. THIS CAN BE AN OPPORTUNITY TO MAKE THINGS MATCH, WHICH OFTEN INCREASES THE FEELING OF HARMONY IN THE ROOM.

BUT KEEP TRYING TO GET A HEADBOARD, ONE THAT REALLY ATTACHES TO THE BED.

Bunk beds are sometimes a necessity in a small room, but don't use them if you can come up with an alternative—perhaps a trundle bed. If bunks are used, try to cover the supports for the upper bunk from the view of the person in the lower bunk. A good choice is dark fabric with a pattern of stars, or maybe fabric that is the child's favorite color. Likewise, if things must be stored under a bed, it's best if they are soft things like bedding or clothes.

Finally, TVs in children's rooms have been scientifically proven to lower the children's IQs. Don't do that to your *keiki*; they are the future and they are likely to need all the intelligence they can get.

> In a bedroom where space is an issue, try to avoid a bunk bed, which has one bed too high and the other too cramped. Try a trundle bed instead.

Entrance Chi

Chi energy comes into a room primarily through the entrance door. Some energy also comes in through windows, depending on how much direct sun they get. There is a **swath of strong *chi*** energy the width of the door going directly across the room from front wall to back wall. See Fig. S. Make sure the bed (or frequently used chair) is not located in that swath of energy—it is too harsh. See Fig. T. If a window is opposite the door, then the *chi* is zooming quickly across the bed and out the window. It is particularly important not to have a bed positioned fully in the swath of *chi* energy with the person's feet facing the door. That's called the "coffin position," because coffins are carried through doorways feet first.

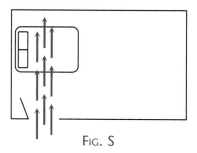

Fig. S

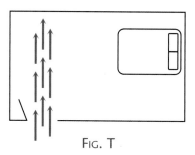

Fig. T

SOLUTIONS

If there is no choice but to have a bed located in that swath of energy, some sort of buffer or screen should be placed between the door and the bed. Here are some examples:

- A large **chest** or armoire, preferably with rounded corners.

- A folding **screen**. Just make sure it's stable.

- Tall, thickly foliaged **plants** (even good artificial ones will do fine).

- A **curtain**. Even sheers will work.

- A **beaded curtain**, if that works with the décor.

- A very thick **rug**, preferably patterned or sculpted.

- A **crystal** or **wind chime** hung between the door and the bed. They symbolize breaking up and slowing down harsh, fast energy.

- A few extra **pillows** are okay in this situation, although in most circumstances you shouldn't have pillows on the bed that are solely for decoration. They're decorative *clutter* at that point.

Any crystal object refracts light and can be used as a symbol of dispersing energy. Here a sparkling crystal paperweight looks quite at home next to an old Rookwood vase.

Opposing Directions

Do not place a **couch directly facing another couch** and do not place a desk directly facing another desk. Such arrangements suggest disagreement because two people could be directly facing each other and thereby have "opposite viewpoints." If rearranging the furniture is not possible, put a crystal between the two people. The crystal can be hung, or a crystal object (such as bowl, vase or paperweight) can be placed on a table. If there is a rug between the two couches (or desks), red string or red tape can be put underneath the rug to indicate a separation. The red line represents new blood and should be parallel to the furniture, as if it were making a *karate* chop between the two pieces. The caution

These couches are directly facing each other and symbolize opposing points of view. Also the bare glass edge of the coffee table has a "cutting energy."

about opposite viewpoints applies only to *couches* and *desks*, not other furniture. Couches and desks are big, and therefore more important.

This crystal candleholder sits on a coffee table between two couches that are directly facing each other. It is symbolically dispersing "opposite energies."

The reality of life on a lovely island is that it can get a bit crowded. If there are extra beds in a bedroom, try to **align head directions**. This is especially important among siblings sleeping in the same room. It symbolizes heads together, in agreement, harmony. If the bed of the main breadwinner(s) of the household is in the same room with other beds, it is the one that should have a solid wall right behind its head. The breadwinners need the good support in their money-earning that this will afford them.

Appliance Locations

The stove is considered to be the most powerful object in the home, because it could conceivably destroy the home. It also represents wealth—your ability to feed people. In all of Polynesia, a person's status was often indicated by the size of *lū'au* they could produce. Gas stovetops are preferred in feng shui over electric stovetops, because the element of fire is then actually present. There are two important issues in the location of the stove in the kitchen: the **ability to see the entrance** into the room, and the relation of the elements **fire and water**. The sink and refrigerator are water. The stove (or microwave or toaster oven) is fire. Fire and water are opposite elements in feng shui. Conflict is common if they are *exactly* next to each other or *directly* across from each other. When they are across from each other and there is an island between them, there is probably not a problem.

SOLUTIONS

• If the stove (oven or range top) is directly across from the refrigerator or sink, hang a **crystal** from the ceiling between the two appliances to symbolize dispersion.

• Put a line of **red tape** or **string** between the fire and water appliances, and *parallel* to them. You are not connecting them, so you do not put the string or tape in the direction that connects them. It's as if you are chopping a red line of separation between them.

If your back is to the kitchen entrance when you are cooking at the stove, use a reflective kettle to see behind you. I never recommend using a mirror at a stovetop, though some people say it brings prosperity. The most important issue is being able to see toward the entrance, and a domed reflective kitchen object (such as a kettle or shiny lid) does the job and looks natural in the location. A mirror behind the stove requires frequent

Below: The dome shape of this shiny kettle acts as a mirror. It looks natural on a stove and lets you see behind your back. This is especially important if your back is to the door. To keep the kettle shiny, don't use an abrasive scrubber.

Built-in microwaves tend to leak more than free-standing ones and should be tested for leakage.

Here, fire and water are too close for even common sense. Imagine the heat of the oven a few inches from the freezer. Their energies are clashing—literally and symbolically.

Finally the fridge front is too cluttered. Don't do that to your fridge (it's harder to clean) and don't do that for your peace of mind.

cleaning and is not likely to show your head fully, especially if there is a range hood or cabinet above the stove—and you don't want your image being chopped off like that.

It's extremely practical to have counter space on each side of the stovetop. But occasionally, even in large kitchens, the refrigerator is exactly next to the stovetop. I've seen scorch marks on the side of the refrigerator. It's poor design and seriously bad feng shui. Moving the appliances is rarely feasible, so use a crystal to symbolically fix the situation. Put the crystal directly above the small gap between the two appliances to disperse their conflicting energies. It can also be put in a cabinet above the refrigerator or stove, as close to the gap as possible. If the refrigerator is built in and surrounded by wood cabinetry, the problem is less severe.

All microwave ovens leak, in my experience. I've tested hundreds, and the built-ins are the worst. Don't stand next to a microwave when it's on, and definitely don't let children stand close, watching things go around inside. Children's cells are dividing at a faster pace than adults' because they are growing. They are therefore more susceptible to radiation damage.

I consulted for a woman who had her mother along to hear what I had to say. The first thing I noticed was a center bathroom, and I gently said, "A center bathroom is a serious problem in feng shui because it is seen as portending disease, divorce or bankruptcy." The mother exclaimed, "That's this house! That's this house!" My client started crying and explained that indeed she and her husband were going through bankruptcy *and* divorce, *and* that she had just been diagnosed with breast cancer. Later when I measured her built-in microwave, it was the leakiest I'd ever measured. I considered it to be a major health issue. There was no place safe in the kitchen when it was turned on. It was directly above the stovetop where she was often tending to food while the microwave was on.

Sharp Corners

Another important rule of furniture placement is this: Don't sit or sleep with a **sharp right angle** pointing at you. Those sharp right angles often come from the vertical edge of furniture. There is a feng shui concept of the "poison arrow," or *shar chi*, which is a sharp or negative energy that is aimed from an angle of 90 degrees or sharper.

Above: This bedside table has a right-angled corner aiming harsh energy across the bed. It is also a few inches too tall. Ideally, bed-side tables should be level with the top of the mattress. Also, all beds need a solid headboard. Only on guest beds is this not important.

Right: The side table has a sharp right angle that causes a poison arrow aimed across the bed.

There is plenty of furniture available with rounded vertical edges. Bamboo, rattan and wicker all feel very right in Hawai'i homes, and their edges are usually rounded. If you cannot replace sharp-edged furniture, cover at least the one sharp corner that aims at you by using cloth or plant leaves.

If the sharp angle is a bedside table, you can stuff an extra pillow between the tabletop and the bed when you are actually in the bed and remove it, if you wish, when you get up.

When I moved into the last apartment I had, over 10 years ago, there was a big, dark Irish armoire from the 1800s right next to my side of the bed. It was built like a fortress, high on both ends and a bit lower in the middle. It made a fierce poison arrow across my side of the bed, and every night we hung a silk robe over the corner. Well, that turned out to be not good enough, because I started having multiple death dreams every night. Nothing like that had ever happened to me, and it really got my attention. I'd wake up at midnight and somebody had just shot me—get back to sleep and wake up at 3:00 because somebody had just stabbed me. The next night somebody would push me off a cliff. It was unrelenting, and I started to be afraid to go to sleep. I wondered if the dreams were portending sickness or death. My partner had inherited the armoire and had no special attachment to it, so we decided to take it to a consignment store and sell it. The very night that the armoire was gone was the first night the dreams stopped, and they have never come back since. You can't fool yourself with dreams; they come to us unbidden.

Sharp angles don't come only from furniture. A wall can jut into the room and make a poison arrow. If that angle points at a bed or at seating that is used a lot, move the furniture, hide the corner with plants or fabric, or "bullnose" the corner with drywall. If you can bullnose it—that is, make it rounded—you will have fixed the problem 100 percent, forever. The poison arrow no longer exists. Energy rolls around the corner harmlessly instead of angling off into the room.

SHAPE IS BASIC

SHAPE IS ONE OF THE MOST IMPORTANT CONSIDERATIONS IN FENG SHUI. IT'S ACTUALLY MORE IMPORTANT THAN COLOR OR MATERIAL. IF IT'S EVENING, AND YOU CAN'T TELL THE COLOR OF AN OBJECT, YOU CAN STILL SEE THE SHAPE OF THE OUTLINE. ODDLY ENOUGH, THE MATERIAL SOMETHING IS MADE OF IS USUALLY THE LEAST IMPORTANT CRITERION FOR DECIDING ABOUT ITS ENERGY. THAT'S BECAUSE YOU OFTEN HAVE TO GET VERY CLOSE TO AN OBJECT AND EXAMINE IT TO BE SURE OF WHAT IT'S MADE OF. "IN THE PERCEPTION OF SHAPE LIES THE BEGINNINGS OF CONCEPT FORMATION," WRITES RUDOLPH ARNHEIM IN HIS MASTERWORK, *VISUAL THINKING*; THEREFORE, MODERN PSYCHOLOGY AGREES THAT SHAPE IS BASIC. IF THE SHAPE IS AT ALL THREATENING (AND FENG SHUI COULD BE CALLED THE *ART* OF PARANOIA) IT'S A GOOD IDEA TO DO SOMETHING ABOUT IT. IMAGINE SOMEONE HOLDING A SHARP PENCIL CLOSE TO YOUR EYE. YOU MIGHT DEVELOP A TWITCH ALTHOUGH IT NEVER TOUCHED YOU. EVEN SUBCONSCIOUSLY, THE BODY IS AWARE WHEN SOMETHING IS POINTED AT IT.

Bare Glass
Edges

These chairs have solid backs, which is good; but the tabletop has a bare glass edge, which represents cutting energy.

Previous: This tabletop has a bare glass edge and is not recommended. Also the chair backs are open and therefore not best for every-day dining.

The bare glass edge of a tabletop or shelf has "cutting energy," according to feng shui. Imagine the bare glass edge projecting into the space until it reaches a person. Imagine that the edge is very sharp. That's exactly how the symbolism works.

If the glass tabletop or shelf does not have a bare edge that extends beyond the surface it's supported on, or if it has a rim around its edge, it is not a problem. So you can have the best of both worlds: You can have the glamour of a glass tabletop and an energetically friendly object at the same time. Such tables are common, and you must insist on them if you want to live with glass tabletops and also have a feng shui-friendly atmosphere. If the glass tabletop is covered with cloth, or even lace, the problem disappears as well.

Glass tabletops are a very modern invention. For most of our history, people have not lived with bare-edged glass tabletops or shelves. You're better off without them, because they can have the severe effect of cutting you off from reaching your goals.

It's best not to get emotionally attached to furniture that has bare glass edges—it is probably not an heirloom. In fact, it's better not to be too attached to *any* furniture or decorative objects. Save your love for living beings—family, friends and pets—things that can love you in return. If you've got some problematic furniture, consider replacing it.

Glass shelves are a problem unless they are in a cabinet. If the cabinet has doors (even glass doors), that helps to keep the cutting vibration of the bare edge out of the room. Any glass shelf with a rim on its edge is not a problem. Rims for glass shelves can be made of bamboo, wood, metal and other materials.

The only time a bare glass edge is acceptable is when the glass is *extremely* thick, at least two and a half to three inches thick. It's better if the thick edge is frosted. Thick glass is very, very heavy, so be sure it's well supported and can't tip over.

There is no cutting energy in this *lānai* arrangement. The glass tabletop does not extend beyond its base, and the vertical edges don't have sharp right angles.

Louvers

The bare glass edge of a louvered (jalousie) window is also a concern. If you regularly sit or sleep close to glass louvers, tilt them so that they are not aimed right at you. This same caution applies to window *coverings* that are louvered, as well. Blinds, both horizontal and vertical, can introduce a sharp energy into the room and should be adjusted so that they aim away from a person's body. This also applies to plantation shutters, but their edges are thicker and duller, so the problem is less severe. ☙

Opposite: The plantation shutters are aimed at the bed, and that's fine as long as no one is *on* the bed.

Left: These plantation shutters are aimed at the chairs, which is fine as long as the chairsare empty.

Right: Now the table is ready for people. The louvers are aimed down, away from the chairs. The dining chairs are excellent because they have solid backs, representing good backing, in decisions and finances. Round dining tables are preferred in feng shui because that shape symbolizes Heaven.

When blinds are turned so they are aimed at a chair, it's not good to sit there on a regular basis. Either adjust them so they aren't aimed at the chair or pull the blinds back.

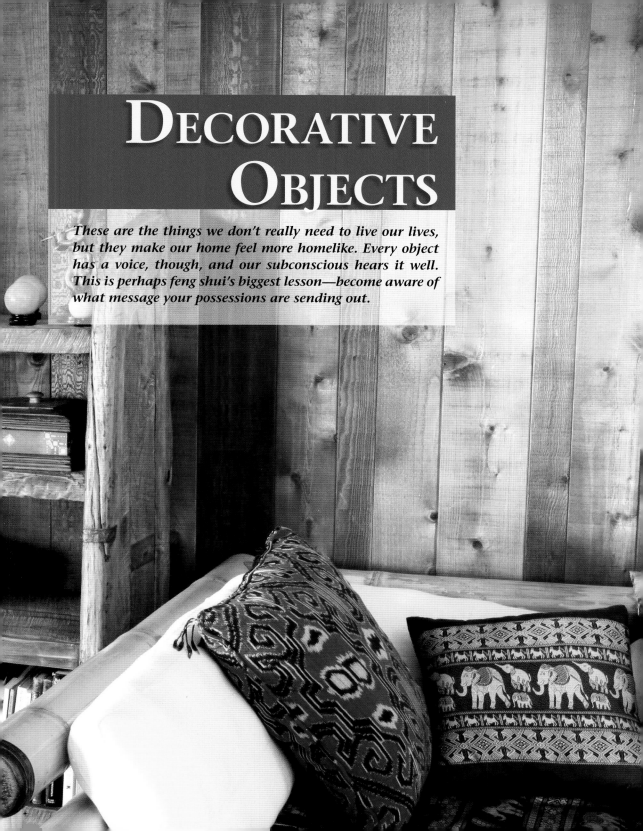

DECORATIVE OBJECTS

These are the things we don't really need to live our lives, but they make our home feel more homelike. Every object has a voice, though, and our subconscious hears it well. This is perhaps feng shui's biggest lesson—become aware of what message your possessions are sending out.

Color

Color, especially wall color, sends big messages in a home. An otherwise plain home can come alive inside with a bit of color. Too much rich dramatic color within a home can say, "Too much *drama* going on." Bold, saturated colors are best used on individual walls or to accent architectural features. Bold colors are not useful in children's rooms. Parents often think that such bright colors will keep the child from being lethargic, but it's best to use milder colors on the walls and bright colors on fabrics which can be more easily changed as the child grows. Bold paint colors are also fine outside as long as they look smart and not ugly. These are the easiest colors to live with *inside*:

• Soft, mild **yellow**. Yellow is a gathering color in feng shui and encourages people to be happy together. Yellow is the happiest color. It's warm without being hot.

• **Green**, like a sage green. This is a mild, greyed-down green and is popular for good reason. Green is a healing color, and I often recommend it for doctor's offices and massage rooms. It's cool without being cold.

• There's nothing wrong with **white**. There are hundreds of different shades of white, and some are better than others. White is usually the best color for ceilings.

• **Grey**, but only in a sunny room, not in a place that's often cloudy.

• **Dusty rose** or old rose. This is a very greyed-down pink. It's one of the few pinks that guys can live with. The place I recommend it is in relationship bedrooms, where a *warm* color symbolizes a warm relationship. Yellow is also fine in relationship bedrooms.

The color I *don't* recommend much inside is blue. It should never be accentuated in the residence of someone who is negative or depressed. It can say, "I've got the blues," especially if it's used a lot. Blue is also too cool to be the predominant color in a relationship bedroom.

Using a **matte** finish inside is preferable. It lets the color be seen more fully without the reflections that come with glossier finishes. Benjamin Moore now makes a technology called Aura that includes a matte finish that's cleanable, so it can be used in bathrooms and kitchens where a glossier finish has been the norm for ease of cleaning. It's expensive, though. It is low-VOC (volatile organic compounds, which are off-gasses that are not good for humans or pets to breathe). Sherwin-Williams also promotes their paint as low-VOC, so there's a positive trend, even among the big companies.

Not Quite Love

Peach or coral are problematic as colors because they're right next to pink (which is the color of love) on the color wheel, but they're not pink and they're not yellow. They're in between. So their feng shui meaning is "I'm in between partners. I'm not quite at the love color. I'm available." They're fine colors to use if you're single and you're looking, but once you've got a ring on your finger, it's best to have less of them in your life.

Maintenance

It's better not to get too attached to material objects—save your love for those who can love you back!

Whatever decorative objects are in your home must be kept dusted and cleaned. If that's too much of a chore in your space, consider *paring down*. Paring down has the extra bonus of *attracting abundance*. Fewer objects in a room say, "There's plenty of room for abundance to pour right in!" If there are too many objects in a room, the message is, "Don't bring anything fresh and wonderful into my life—I wouldn't have a place to put it."

Fresh energy represents new opportunities in your life. The best way to welcome fresh energy into a home is to keep it clean. Old dust and dirt hold old vibrations. Cleaning is always a noble act: It is like a physical prayer when done mindfully. The best way to clean a place well is with no audio distraction such as music, radio or TV.

I can only recall once when a house was *too clean*. It was *mauka* of Hilo and rather cool, and the client said, "When my friends come over they say my place feels cold." I just blurted out my first response: "Sterile is the word." I wish hospitals were that clean. She confessed that her husband thought she was crazy because she would start scrubbing a perfectly clean floor right in the middle of watching a TV show. I diplomatically suggested that she not be such a perfectionist.

Don't have too many broken things in and around your home, waiting to be fixed in the mythical by-and-by. Broken things say "breaking up" and don't bode well for relationships. When I see a lot of broken things in a home I start humming that old song, "Breaking Up Is Hard to Do," and after a while I sing it and after a while they get it.

A CLEAN SWEEP

YES, IT'S AS SIMPLE AS IT SEEMS—IF YOU'RE FEELING STUCK IN YOUR LIFE, START CLEANING. LOOK AROUND YOUR HOME WITH AWARENESS AND A WILLING ATTITUDE, AND SEE WHAT NEEDS SOME CLEANING. IF YOU FIND YOURSELF CLEANING AN OBJECT THAT DOESN'T WORK, REPAIR IT OR DONATE IT. TRUST THAT SOMETHING BETTER WILL COME ALONG. YOU'LL TESTIFY TO THE JOYS OF A CLUTTER-FREE LIFE.

Water Pictures and Water Features

The water in this picture is moving toward the left, so it shouldn't be placed to the right of the door (inside). This kind of picture is perfect for the left side of the door because it would symbolize water flowing from the door into the home.

Water symbolizes money or prosperity in any form. **Water pictures** can be useful in feng shui to symbolize bounty. Remember, *waiwai* is the Hawaiian word for wealth. A waterfall picture on the entrance wall inside your home can be a good thing. But it can also be a very bad thing, depending on the relationship between the position of the door and the direction of water flow in the picture. The water should not be flowing toward the front door, and thus toward the outside of the home. That would symbolize money leaving the home. When the water is flowing to the left, don't put that picture to the right of the door. It would work best to the left—that way, it symbolizes money flowing through the door into your home. If the final flow of the water depicted is simply vertical, it can go on either side of the front door—on the inside.

A **water feature** is any decorative object that features real water. The most common kind is a small electric fountain. If you have one of these on display, you must keep it running. Otherwise, it's doing more harm than good, by sending the wrong message: "Dried up—broken." It's fine to have the fountain turned off when you are sleeping or gone for the day, but it is preferable that it be on when you arrive home, so use a timer if necessary. If the water flows in only one direction, that direction should be toward the center of the room. That way the "abundance" is flowing in toward you, not just away from you. If you have a fountain that flows in all directions, it doesn't matter as much where it is placed. Generally, don't put a fountain next to a stove or microwave oven. That's putting fire and water too close together, and it can symbolize argument.

Patterns and Images

There are two patterns that feng shui cautions against: bold stripes and lone images. Lone images can signify aloneness, and bold stripes can signify argument. Subtle stripes are fine, but if the stripes are vivid, like cabana stripes, the symbolism implies that one person's opinion is one stripe, and another person's opinion is another stripe. They don't come together; they stay separate, as separate pathways.

Barkcloth in vintage tropical patterns looks quite at home in Hawai'i. The images within this pattern relate beautifully to each other.

Here's a good example of "relationship energy": a pair of sculptures under a painting of several *ti* plants. There are even two drawers.

Lone images come and go in design fashion. Single palms are a current trend, but they say "aloneness." Even on a large piece of fabric like a shower curtain, they don't relate to each other. They are not in groups, as palms often are in nature. They're just a repeated image of a lone palm. Vintage barkcloth is just one example of a tropical-looking fabric that says, instead, "relationship."

Very often I am called to the homes of a single person who hopes the consultation can help them find a partner. I look around the home and usually see numerous images of single people, such as a lone *hula* dancer. Usually the images are the same gender as the occupant. The message these people are putting out to the Universe is that they want to be single, and sure enough they are. A few lone images can be all right, but don't have a preponderance of them. If you're single and looking for a partner, avoid lone images—except one. That one should be just outside your front door. If you're looking for a man, put a male image to the right of your front door (as you stand outside, facing the door). If you're looking for a woman, put a female image to the left of the door. The right side is the dragon (masculine) side, and the left is the tiger (feminine) side. I think of it as feng shui advertising.

A few years ago I was helping a friend get rid of single images in her home, so she could get a boyfriend. She lives in an apartment, so we had to be subtle about the masculine image outside her door. I gave her a Duke Kahanamoku postage stamp that I had in my notebook, and she put it up immediately. (There's a lot of power in doing something immediately.) It wasn't long before she was on the phone to me, singing the praises of her hunky new boyfriend—"So sexy, so masculine…" I'm thinking to myself, "That's what I would expect, using a Duke image."

There are other things to watch for besides single images. If you use a fabric with a bold, attention-getting pattern, don't use other patterns that are just as bold in the same room. Use solid colors, or subtle patterns such as damask. Too many bold, different patterns in the same room amount to visual clutter and confuse *chi* energy. Your attention is jerked around chaotically.

Most of the artwork I see in Hawai'i is representational, not abstract. If abstract art is used, it should not elicit feelings of chaos, confusion or conflict. They are not appropriate in private homes, where serenity and harmony should reign.

One of the most important places for a nice view or wall art is at the foot of a person's bed. If it's a relationship bed, both people need to like what they see. That view, often the first thing that's seen in the morning, represents the future, because it's what you open your eyes to. So if a picture is hanging there, *both* people need to like it. Bedrooms are not best served with pictures of people or animals with their eyes open. I feng shui'd in a child's bedroom that had a huge collection of Beanie Babies on very high shelf, all looking

This peaceful Pele face, designed by Herb Kawainui Kane, is a beautiful example of a feminine image wall sculpture.

expectantly at the bed. I asked the parents, "How well does he sleep in here?" They replied, "Oh, he can't sleep in here at all. He sleeps with us." I said, "Well, I couldn't sleep in here either, with all those eyes wide open." I recommended covering them at night, and moving them lower in the room if possible. Heavy things (and this looked like a collection of every kind of Beanie Baby ever made) on a high shelf are considered to be foreboding.

We close our eyes at night—but it's harder to do when objects or pictures are staring at us.

Mirrors

Mirrors are often recommended in feng shui, but there are several important cautions concerning them:

• Any adult needs to be able to see their head fully in any mirror in their home, from the voice box to the top of the head, and preferably eight inches above their head. This doesn't apply to the tiny dime-size mirrors used as feng shui solutions.

• Don't split up reflected images with mirror tiles. This also applies to the trend of putting mirrors in window frames with the mullions dividing up the glass. Those kinds of mirrors are fine if placed high enough so that no one sees themselves reflected.

• Don't use a mirror of smoked or colored glass in places where a person could see themselves in it. The same is true for a mirror with words or images etched into the glass.

• Don't show these things in a mirror:

  ⊙ Clutter. There would dauntingly seem to be more of it.
  ⊙ A toilet. Then there would be two of the most problematic object in the home.
  ⊙ The bottoms of stairs alone. If a mirror is going to reflect just part of stairs, it shouldn't be just the bottom, because that signifies lower energy.
  ⊙ Another mirror directly across, because this reflection is seen as crazy and chaotic.

Mirrors in the bedroom are controversial in feng shui. Some experts say they're great and some say they're not. I say, "How well do you sleep?" If everyone in the room sleeps soundly, no worries. If somebody doesn't sleep well, put curtains over the mirrors at night to make a quieter, more *yin* atmosphere. The curtains can be open during the day. The least preferable place for a mirror in the bedroom is at the foot of the bed. If it's there already and you can't move it, consider putting a *pareu* or other fabric drape over it when you're sleeping. Again, use your judgment, based on how well you rest. My motto is, if it ain't broke, don't fix it.

It's good to have a mirror reflecting the dining table, because it symbolically doubles the bounty. Just make sure that peoples' heads are shown fully both when seated and standing. From a design point of view, mirrors are best placed where they bring a view of nature onto a wall—like another window in the room. Mirrors are seen to expand a space in feng shui, and thereby they keep your life from being too closed up. Use them all you want, but just follow the above rules and keep the glass clean. If you let the cleaning liquid reach the very bottom of the mirror glass, it will wick under and around to the back side, and over time will cause dark blotches in the silvering along the bottom.

The large mirror above the couch reflects an outside view and seems like a window, thereby expanding the energy in a narrow room.

Plants

Dried plants represent stagnant energy in feng shui. This is because they were once alive and had sap flowing through them, but now they do not. That source of *chi* energy is cut off, and they're getting drier and deader by the minute.

Items *made* of dead plants, such as wood furniture and *lauhala* mats, are not a problem. This is because they have been formed into useful objects. The purpose of a dried plant arrangement is to simply preserve the plant form, which is no longer functional. Those particular plants were once alive, and now they're quite dead. What about something like a palm-sheaf basket with dried flowers glued onto it, which I saw recently? I suggest carefully removing the dried flowers—and making sure you actually use the basket. *Using* the basket is a new concept for some people! And what about lampshades or other paper products with real, dried leaves pressed into them? I recommend getting rid of them.

Artificial plants are not a problem because they were never alive. They just *represent* living plants. Take the time to arrange the foliage realistically, and keep them very clean.

Paper made with pressed flower petals or leaves is popular nowadays—but it's bad feng shui. These plants were alive, but now they're dead.

The caution about dried plants applies to arrangements, potpourri, wreaths and *lei*. Any dried plants can be kept on display for a season. If the dried plant is being kept for sentimental reasons (such as a *lei* from a special occasion), pack it away after about three months. *Lei* made of seeds, shells, feathers, or paper or artificial flowers may be on display indefinitely as long as they are kept dusted.

I feng shui'd for a recently married couple who bickered constantly throughout the consultation. Above their bed was their framed wedding bouquet. It was certainly not helping to keep their marriage alive and loving. I suggested that they put it away, hoping they would do so before their marriage became as dead as the flowers.

Living plants enliven a space in a very special way, because they're actually alive and growing. If you choose to keep live plants in your home, they must be and look healthy. A diseased or dying plant is bringing exactly that kind of energy into your space. Two trouble-free plants that I often recommend are peace lily (*Spathiphyllum*) and lady palm (*Rhapis*). Lucky bamboo (*Dracaena sanderiana*) is also an easy-to-grow plant, but it's not actually a bamboo, and the only thing lucky about it is that you can't kill it. In general, don't have houseplants with stiff, pointed leaves. *Sansevieria trifasciata* (mother-in-law's tongue) is an exception because the leaves point directly upward and not out toward people.

Orchids are among the most evolved plants on earth. When they are flowering they are stunning, natural works art. But when they're not in bloom, they can be plain ugly. Many people keep them on a *lānai* between flowerings, but if you don't have that option, consider getting a single artificial orchid sprig and sticking it in with the plant.

The lovely peace lily (*Spathiphylum wallissi*) practically thrives on neglect.

LIVING JEWELS

THERE'S A CATEGORY OF ORCHIDS CALLED JEWEL ORCHIDS, SEVERAL GENERA OF WHICH HAVE EXQUISITELY VARIEGATED LEAVES THAT SPARKLE IN SUNLIGHT. ONE JEWEL ORCHID (*LUDISIA DISCOLOR*) HAS PURPLE LEAVES VARIEGATED WITH FINE PINK LINES. IT IS CONSIDERED BY SOME TO BE THE MOST BEAUTIFUL LEAF IN NATURE. THIS GROUND ORCHID SOMEWHAT RESEMBLES A PURPLE WANDERING JEW PLANT, AND IT IS JUST AS EASY TO GROW. IT MAKES A LOVELY AND UNDEMANDING HOUSEPLANT.

Directing *Chi* Energy

Previous: If the walking sticks and umbrellas were just standing on the floor, they would be directing energy down and out of the home. Because they are in a basket, the energy is contained, and all is well.

Any stick that has one end on the floor and the other end resting against a wall counts as a "stick going down" because that's just what it is. It can be big bamboo, a simple yardstick, a broom or mop, or just a board left there for no good reason. Put its bottom end in a container such as a basket, box or pot. Hang brooms and mops (they'll last longer that way, too). Otherwise, store stick-like items horizontally.

The reason this is an issue is that the eye sees the stick close to eye-level, then follows it down to the floor. The eye is drawn down, and *chi* is considered also to go down and out.

The opposite of letting *chi* flow down and out is pulling it up in a room. There are very many ways to do this. You are only limited by your imagination with this one, because for the most part all you're doing is drawing the eye upward—straight up or at an angle. Here are some examples:

• **Drapes that puddle**. Extra fabric puddles on the floor, with a feeling of lushness and romance. Any low *chi* gets drawn to the complicated pile of fabric on the floor, then follows one of the folds up. Your eye does the same thing. I can recommend this only for homes that are fairly clean, and without indoor pets. If the floor is dirty, the fabric will get dirty at the bottom, and that's no good. This is certainly not a solution for everyone.

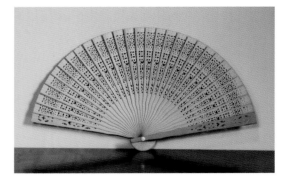

• A decorative **fan** as a wall ornament. *Chi* moves from the fan's wide direction in the same way a breeze is generated by fanning yourself. This can be used near stairs to direct people up or down, whichever direction you'd prefer them to go.

This sandalwood fan can be used as a wall ornament. In this position, it moves energy mostly upward.

• **Objects at an angle** along a wall. In order to draw energy up and not down, the lowest object should usually be fairly close to eye level, definitely not below waist level. For that reason, this technique is often best used in rooms with high ceilings.

• **Ceiling shadows** in the evening. The shadows must not look weird—that's important. I prefer palm leaf shadows and especially appreciate it when they softly move. Clear bulbs (in uplights) are best for distinct shadows.

You can also direct energy across a room in a certain direction by placing a rug (or rugs) at an angle to the wall. This works best, by far, with rectangular rugs that have fringe on the two short ends. The fringe directs you to step on and off at those ends. Angling rugs or furniture, or just about anything in a room, enlivens the room and makes it a bit more *yang*.

There is nothing weird about palm leaf shadows. They are instantly recognizable and add enchantment to a space. Be sure to use a clear bulb for more distinct shadows.

Gifts

The main problem with decorative objects is having too many. In Hawai'i, that can come from too much gift receiving. Do not keep any object just because someone gave it to you. Keep it because it is genuinely useful in your life, and/or because you genuinely enjoy having the object around. If you are on the receiving end of culturally expected gift-giving, and you aren't fond of the gift, don't keep it. It's as simple as that. It's your home, not anyone else's. You do your own decorating with objects that feel harmonious to you. If you are keeping objects on display because so-and-so might come over by-and-by, and might wonder why their gift is not on display, then the object is a "guilt gift." You'd feel guilty if that gift weren't on display in your home. You are giving the gift-giver too much power in your home and in your life. Offer the object back to them, or pass it on to someone else.

Keeping "guilt gifts" conveys a squelched vibration to the home. The home is struggling to support you, but it can't quite do it. It's as if you're trying to wear other people's clothing that is the wrong size and style. By letting go of such objects, you are opening up wellsprings of fresh energy into your life. A freshly cleared surface is a big signal to the Universe to bring in new opportunities. Remember, don't ever let decorative objects squeeze you out of usable space in your home.

If you are the one who's giving gifts, consider delicious, nutritious food or long-lasting tropical flowers, such as orchids, protea or anthuriums. Such gifts will never become a burden to the receiver. If you give food, they can eat it; if you give flowers, they can enjoy arranging them and won't have to be bothered dusting them off for years.

Only occasionally do I see homes with too few decorative objects. Such homes feel barren, awkward and cold. The solution to this is simple: Add a few objects that have meaning to you and bring beauty and good energy into your home. Consider shopping at yard sales or online if you don't care

If you've received a gift that's not your style, don't feel obligated to keep it. Beware of letting your home get cluttered with objects that don't reflect you. Remember, each object has a voice.

for conventional stores. Of course, it is possible to get by with almost no decorative objects and still have the home feel balanced. The Japanese have done so for centuries. But this is a very careful, studied style. The bareness is integral and in no way haphazard. The modern decorating style called Minimalism also demonstrates a sparse use of objects within a stylish décor. It requires discipline and plenty of closets to accomplish it well.

SUGAR-FREE DECORATING

IF SOMEONE IN THE HOME HAS DIABETES, WATCH OUT FOR TOO MANY SMALL, "SWEET" OBJECTS ON DISPLAY—THEY ARE LIKE GRAINS OF SUGAR. AFTER ALL, DIABETES USED TO BE CALLED "SUGAR DIABETES." LOOK FOR LARGER DECORATIVE OBJECTS, AND FEWER OF THEM.

Clutter

I saved this section for last, and I'll be gentle, but the truth is, "Clutter stops everything!" Be especially careful not to let clutter accumulate in corners, where it sometimes seems prone to gather. Corners are powerful places; don't let things stagnate there. Don't leave holiday stuff up year-round; it's holding you back in the past. Ditto for clocks that don't work and calendars that aren't up-to-date.

I firmly believe clutter is bad for your health. People have often come up after my classes and asked what they could do for a friend or relative who has cancer. I first ask, "Is there clutter?" Every time, they say yes, indicating that it's pretty severe clutter. A gentleman I knew had a nice home, but it was filled with the worst and most obsessive clutter I'd ever seen. In every room of the house there were pathways through the clutter going from door to door. Right next to his dining chair was a stack of *National Enquirer* newspapers that was three decades old, with notes on the front covers telling the page numbers of the important articles! I said, "Let's recycle them." He answered, "No, I'm going to give them to a friend." I said he should go ahead and give them away. "My friend doesn't want them," he replied and then changed the subject. It was difficult to *circulate* in his home, and his biggest health problem involved circulation. Soon afterward, he drove himself to a hospital because he felt he was having heart problems. He had a heart attack on the steps going into the hospital and died the next day.

Clearing clutter (and especially paper clutter) is one of the most emotionally wrenching things that you can do if you're really stuck. So pack 'um away now and put off the pain 'til later! Make decisions about whether or not to keep certain items at a time that suits you. For now just label your boxes well and put them away wherever you can, even if that means just covering the boxes with nice fabric for a while. Putting things away now is a good way to learn which of your possessions you really miss seeing or using. Well, bring those items that you miss back out and see how nice they look without the other clutter around them. You can clear clutter in one big swoop or take it a bit at a time. If you do it a bit at a time, make sure you do it *daily*, even if it's just 15 minutes a day.

What if you're living in a cluttered house, but you're not the one who is generating the clutter? The clutter is still affecting you and everyone living there. Be persistent, be helpful, bribe the generator of the clutter, do whatever it takes. It may take perseverance, but don't let up (in a nice way). Nobody wants to live in clutter and see their nice things not look their best because it's too much trouble to keep them clean. But also nobody wants to live with a nag, so beware of the fine line, and stay positive. 🍃

Reduce, reuse and recycle to keep the *'āina* and ocean clean and healthy. It's good to occasionally reevaluate the items in your home. Maybe some of them are just "old news."

Recommended Books

On Feng Shui

There are more than 500 feng shui books in English. Some are better than others. I review and rate books on my website, fungshway.com—mostly books on feng shui and related topics such as tropical horticulture. My previous books are *Feng Shui Demystified* and *Bedroom Feng Shui*. I do recommend both of them. If your local store doesn't have them, try bookfinder.com. (I like it as well as, if not better than, Amazon, because it *includes* Amazon.) Also look for my forthcoming book, *Feng Shui for Hawai'i Gardens*.

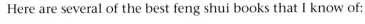

Here are several of the best feng shui books that I know of:

Lighting the Eye of the Dragon by *Baolin Wu*
Stands head and shoulders above most feng shui books. In it a great master reveals rare wisdom.

Feng Shui and Your Health by *Dr. Jess Lim*
Very traditional and extraordinarily thorough.

Feng Shui and Health by *Nancy Santopietro*
Brilliant—a true masterpiece. It has an excellent explanation of split views, and there are amazing case histories.

Feng Shui for Dummies by *David Kennedy*
A uniquely complete book. It is actually the most complete feng shui book I've seen.

Choose the Best House for You by *Elliot Tanzer*
Almost as complete, and you don't have to put up with the
"cutesiness" of the Dummies series, which is not to everyone's taste.

Any book written by Eva Wong
Top-notch. She covers both Landform and Compass Schools,
which most books don't. I'm a Landform practitioner, and
can say with assurance that her words, insights and illustra-
tions on Landform are not found elsewhere. Eva Wong is one
of the greatest feng shui writers.

Feng Shui: Art and Harmony of Place
by *Johndennis Govert*
Wonderfully understandable book, and he's not afraid to
say what he thinks: for instance, "People who live in glass
houses shouldn't."

Feng Shui House Book by *Gina Lazenby*
A lavish and very beautiful book. She uses color photographs
to educate, which served as my inspiration for the photos and
captions in this book.

Practical Feng Shui by *Simon Brown*
This is perhaps Simon Brown's best feng shui book. The Compass School is famous for being complicated, but he guides
you right along.

Quick Feng Shui Cures by *Sarah Shurety*
A unique book. She actually tells you what to do with all the
different feng shui lucky charms that are available in China-
town. I'm not a great fan of lucky charms, but lots of people
are. If you've got them, it's good to know what they mean.

On Home Care

Your home supports you best when it is clean and organized. If that's a challenge for you, read these fine books:

Jeff Campbell has written three of the best books on home cleaning and care. **Speed Cleaning** explains what you should try to do every week or two—at least every month. **Spring Cleaning** has the best window-cleaning instructions I've ever seen, as well as much more. **Good as New** explains how to fix common things. Repairing and reusing are important for the planet, and they're just good common sense.

Clear Your Clutter with Feng Shui by *Karen Kingston*
Has all the motivation you'll ever need to declutter.

Getting Things Done by *David Allen*
Could change your life if you are a disorganized person. There are many things to do in Hawai'i, and Allen shows how to take the stress out of being productive. It has my highest recommendation.

Electromagnetic Fields by *Blake Levitt*
This is a wake-up call. It explains where EMFs occur and which illnesses may have a strong connection to them. The early Chinese didn't have to deal with this modern, invisible pollution, and neither did the ancient Hawaiians, but it is here and now in several places in most homes these days. Modern feng shui consultants usually have a gauss meter to measure for EMFs.

Straight Talk on Decorating by *Lynette Jenning*
Here's one decorating book that I recommend all the time when someone is interested in painting their interior walls. Her color charting system on page 129 is brilliant for showing how to use interesting color and still keep a harmonious and tied-together feeling.

On Hawaiian Culture

Not many books mention *kuhikuhi pu'uone*, the ancient Hawaiian consultants on house placement and contouring. Here are a few that do:

The Polynesian Family System in Ka'ū, Hawai'i
by *Craighill Handy and Mary Kawena Pukui*
A truly marvelous book. The authors offer examples of what the *kuhikuhi pu'uone* taught and how it was good common sense, not superstition. The whole second paragraph on page 8 could have been lifted from a feng shui book, offering such advice as "A home should not stand at the base of a cliff" and "The entry should have light and no obstructions."

Ancient Hawaiian Life by *Edwin Bryan*
Short but covers a huge variety of subjects, including the home.

Ka Po'e Kahiko: The People of Old by *Samuel Kamakau* and Hawaiian Antiquities by *David Malo*
Both are very great classics and also mention *kuhikuhi pu'uone*.

Ancient Hawaiian Civilization by *Craighill Handy, Peter Buck and others*
Unique in that it refers to the *kilokilo*, not the *kuhikuhi pu'uone*, as being the diviner who was consulted as to the house and its location. The information found in "Beliefs Concerning the New House," "Building the House" and "Consecrating the House" is fascinating. The book even covers which direction the people slept in—with their heads toward the central pillar (*halakea* or *pou manu*).

Hawaiian Dictionary
by *Mary Pukui and Samuel Elbert*
Should be proudly on display in every home in Hawai'i (in my opinion). The hardback has a beautiful red cloth cover, and its very presence helps to keep the language alive. It really does.

Below: Pukui's books in red bindings; one is cotton and the other is fine silk. These quality bindings echo the excellent quality information within, and the crystal bookends symbolize dispersing energy. May the knowledge in these books continue to be spread throughout the land.

Glossary

Bullnose Corners

These are long plastic premolded drywall beads that make a curve instead of a sharp right angle. They are applied after the sheetrock but before the mudding. Check stores that sell drywall supplies.

Chi

The Chinese word for energy of any kind—visible or invisible. It is spelled *qi* in the *Pin-yin* Romanization scheme. The Japanese transliteration is *ki.*

Crystal

The best crystals for feng shui solutions are completely clear, not tinted or iridescent. Manufactured "lead-glass crystal," or natural "from-the-earth" crystals can both be used. Clear crystals are preferable because they form the best rainbows in sunlight. Rainbows are formed when light is dispersed into bands. That's why crystals symbolize dispersion.

You can use cut-crystal objects such as paperweights, bowls or vases. The best shapes for crystals that hang are either a disco-ball shape or an octagon. Generally speaking, don't hang crystals that point down sharply. The octagonal shape is preferred where there's sunlight, because it forms the largest and most distinct patches of color. Be careful: If a crystal is hung so it bumps against regular window glass, the crystal can be easily chipped. Leaded crystal is softer than regular glass because it has a higher lead content. If a natural crystal is used, it should be clear or have rainbow rutilations.

Elements

In Taoism, there are considered to be five elements: Water, Wood, Fire, Metal and Earth. They represent *archetypal energies* that can be used to classify anything.

I Ching

The *I Ching* is an ancient Chinese oracle, considered by many to be the oldest book in the world. There are many excellent translations, but my favorite is *The Book of Changes and the Unchanging Truth* by Ni Hua Ching. It's like a wise old friend who explains the bigger picture when you find yourself stuck in circular and unproductive thinking.

Mirror, *Bagua*

A mirror with an eight-sided frame, with the *I Ching* trigrams around the eight sides. If it doesn't have the trigrams, it's just an octagonal mirror and not a *bagua* mirror. A mirror with the Chinese animals around it is also not a *bagua* mirror.

Some *bagua* mirrors have a blue-tinted plastic film sticking to the glass when you buy them. The film is to protect the glass before purchase, so please remove it before using the mirror. Otherwise, it will be much less effective.

Only use a *bagua* mirror when you really need it. It shouldn't be used to "bring in good energy." It is a mirror; it reflects away. These mirrors symbolize everything being in good order and are considered to be powerful. Don't use them inside your home, except in a very few circumstances (i.e., for a center bathroom or for interior stairs facing the front door). They are primarily for use outside. They are available at Chinese dry goods stores.

A Seal of Solomon mirror is also acceptable instead of a *bagua* mirror in all cases. They both represent perfect order and balance. The Seal of Solomon is from the Bible and has also been used in Hinduism. You may have to make your own with paint or a marker.

Mirror, Concave

Concave mirrors "cave in"—curve inward. They enlarge a very close image, but turn a distant image upside down. This makes the distant object less important. Use it outside when a large or tall object (such as the *pali* or a large building) dwarfs your structure. Concave mirrors absorb harmful energy. See Fig. B on page 30.

Mirror, Convex

Convex mirrors bulge outward. They reflect and disperse energy from many directions. They're available where auto supplies are sold. See Fig. A on page 30.

Mirror, Small Flat

These dime- or quarter-size mirrors are inexpensive and readily available in craft-supply stores. They can be discreetly used to symbolically push energy directly back to the source of the problem.

Poison Arrow

This negative *chi* energy is called *sha* or *shar chi* in Chinese. It is *chi* energy that has encountered something in the environment (such as a long straight line) that causes it to speed up or get irritated.

Solution

This is something that provides a remedy, cure or adjustment. It's whatever feng shui can suggest in order to help the situation. A solution can be real or symbolic. A real solution is a physical change that eliminates the problem—this is the ideal outcome.

A symbolic solution is just a symbol of your intention. It can be made more powerful by saying out loud why you're doing it. You only need to say it once, at the moment when you implement the solution. You can use more than one solution if it feels appropriate.

Wind Chime

Like a crystal, a wind chime is a symbol of energy being dispersed, because it takes the energy of the wind and disperses it into musical notes. It can be used instead of a hanging crystal in any of the solutions. Unless they are small, though, they can look awkward indoors. If a wind chime is heard, you should like the sound; otherwise, replace it.

Yin/Yang

These are the two fundamental categories for classifying all energies and entities in the Universe, according to ancient Chinese Taoism. Nothing is totally *yin* or totally *yang*; rather, things fall on a scale of more *yin* or more *yang*.

YIN	YANG
Dirty	*Clean*
Cluttered	*Uncluttered*
Complex	*Simple*
Slow	*Fast*
Dead	*Alive*
Passive	*Active*
Black	*White*
Dark	*Light*
Horizontal	*Vertical*
Asleep	*Awake*
Stagnant	*Moving*
Wet	*Dry*
Cold	*Hot*
Soft	*Hard*
Private	*Public*
Quiet	*Noisy*
Lower	*Upper*

The *yin/yang* symbol shows that in everything resides a seed of its opposite. The important thing to do is keep things in balance.

This is the classic orientation—turning clockwise, with *yang* up. Sometimes red is used instead of white, because red symbolizes fire—the most *yang* element.

Sources

Pele Mask wall sculpture — Mary Ann Hylton, islandstudios@sgaprod.com

Green Man wall sculpture — Art Farm, 808-323-3495, 82-6159 Māmalahoa Highway, Captain Cook, HI 96704

Brilliant red flowerpots — (high-quality, made in California) Anuenue Gardens, 808-324-4769, 79-7372 Māmalahoa Highway, Kealakekua, HI 96750, Anuenuegardens.com

Tiny indoor wind chimes — Kona Stories, 808-324-0350, 79-7460 Māmalahoa Highway, Kainaliu, HI 96750, konastories.com

Tiny round mirrors — Craft stores usually have packages of 10 for less than $2.00. If your local Ben Franklin doesn't have them in stock, they can get them. Order Darice Mirrors #1613-41 or #1633-82.

Sheer curtains (the Fern pattern on page 45) — Christina Birtcher, luv2reuse@aol.com

Polynesian fabrics — Kapa Fabrics, 808-329-1114, Kona Plaza D2, 75-5719 Ali'i Drive, Kailua-Kona, HI 96740, kapafabrics.com

Quake Wax, 800-959-4953, earthquakeinfo.com
Museum Gel, 800-634-6932, conservationresources.com
These are two of the best brands of sticky wax, used by museums, to hold down breakable objects. The wax is completely removable with Goo Gone or something similar. Using it can save heirlooms and other valuable possessions from falling and breaking during an earthquake.

Retail, World of Feng Shui, Inc., 808-739-8288, 1020 Kapahulu Ave., Honolulu, HI 96816 and 808-487-3888, Pearlridge Center (Uptown), 98-1005 Moanalua Rd., Aiea, HI 96701

Acknowledgments

I gratefully thank and acknowledge Steve Mann for photography and typing, Rick Mears for drawings, Christine and David Reed for being understanding and George Engebretson and Marisa Oshiro of Watermark Publishing for being a pleasure to work with.

I give a special thanks to those who allowed their homes and gardens to be photographed: Bettye Best, Susan Brokaw, Margaret Krimm, Marty and Robert Dean, Dianne and Jon Doherty, Bethann and Don Duval, Kahawai o Kohala, Rita-Oceania K. Mark, Barbara and Rob Kildow, Ira Ono, Sharon Paoa and Lori Honl, Louis Spielman, Roger and Lydia Weiss, Henry Williams, Barbara Cherner and Michael Heyer, Norma Rawlins and Alicia Zee, Tom Sorensen and Paul Endresen, Alysee and Larry Catron, Helen and L. O. Harding, Edwina and Avery Simmons, Christina Birtcher and Amy Ferguson. *Mahalo* to Herb Kawainue Kane for the Pele Mask design and to Mary Ann Hylton for the production of it.

Photo Credits

Index

About the Author

A professional member of the International Feng Shui Guild, Clear Englebert has taught feng shui in Hawai'i and California and consults on homes, gardens and commercial spaces throughout the Islands. He is also the author of *Feng Shui Demystified* and *Bedroom Feng Shui*, which have appeared in four languages. Visit www.fungshway.com.